# Easy Book of Focus

## Wrestle Back Your Focus From Chaos

## Amit Verma

**Author of Easy Book Of Thoughts**

INDIA · SINGAPORE · MALAYSIA

ISBN
Paperback  979-8-89556-623-7
Hardcase  979-8-89588-362-4

# INDEX

Dedication

Dedicated to the person who has always acted as
a silent bulletproof shield for me (my father)

# WRITING A USEFUL BOOK

I have written one more book earlier. The aim was to present an important concept in an enjoyable and graspable way. The first book was *Easy Book of Thoughts*, and it was well received by my friends all over the planet. This gave me the courage to write this one.

A brief idea about an easy book of..... series for you.

I read a lot of books. Whenever I read a non-fiction book, I like a few aspects of it. A good non-fiction book is expected to have the following features.

It should have a readable font.

It should tell a good story with the essence of the message visible to the reader.

Important information should appear at the beginning.

It should have a balance of rational and emotional, real and abstract.

There should be clever headlines.

It should be simple but not amateur.

It should be well-trimmed.

It should have visuals to tell the story.

It should evoke at least one of the emotions in the reader.

I have tried to install these features in my books in the *Easy Book* series.

Hope you observe these as you go through.

It should be like you are being told things by your wise mentor friend after he has just finished his strong coffee.

# PROLOGUE

**Why I wrote this book!**

**"Time is the fire in which we burn"**
**– Delmore Schwartz**

Every book has a starting point. During the last 5-6 years, I have seen this very closely. You can put a camera in any home in India, and you will see similar themes unfolding everywhere.

A wise old man who had only a newspaper to distract him from his family and work, but now he has a screen.

It wakes him up. It fills him with rage when misinformation and political propaganda are served as news. He listens to the useless and endless things wrapped in short videos with no positive consequence.

He sits in one corner of the bed in one corner of the room. He hardly notices the family moving around him and the guests sitting in front.

His views have become more polarised and concrete. He is always angry beneath the surface of aloofness.

Now, let's see his other family members.

Mother watches a spiritual guru with a gigantic empire to instill religious fanaticism slowly on his YouTube channel with a big QR code for donations.

Kids spy and wait to get a chance to see that screen throughout the day. Their childhood is passing without touching the soil, leaves, and butterflies and ladybugs. The video games and horror shorts swamp their innocent minds.

Wife watches reels and the latest clothes as she winds up the day. Talks of a couple about life and the future are pushed back in the context. Things simmer and worsen before someone picks them up with tired eyes or while charging the phone.

Husband watches book reels and car mileage or memes and similar things that were best done offline in the good old days.

Little kids aged 4-5 years wait for lunchtime and dinnertime to get a chance to watch television or use a phone. In between, they choke on accumulated bites in their cheeks, and their eyes are soggy and dry.

Among these, a family is slowly drifting apart.

I want to see those old men who saw things around them and kids who moved and tinkered with things.

Kids who used to learn from real humans and not from influencers; now get brainwashed by the madness of social media trends.

I want to see technology stop turning society insane. But it might be too late!

# PROLOGUE 2

**"You become what you give your attention to."**
**– Epictetus**

Let's start with a little story. It is a small creature which resembles humans. It is lazy and prefers to lie on a flat soft surface for the maximum time possible. It can eat prey double its size like us humans who gorge on huge living and non-living things.

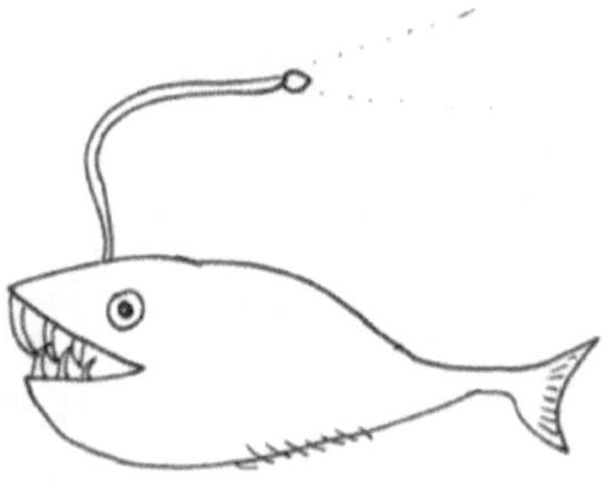

**Angler fish**

It belongs to the teleost genus. It differs from us due to the fact that in this species males are smaller than females and hence cannot boss them with their overconfidence.

It has a unique organ. It produces light which very few enlightened humans produce. Actually, it has even smaller creatures (bacteria) which help it in producing light. Light helps it capture its food.

**Angler fish** are very similar to humans. Like us, it has a lazy body, and it focuses all its light on its fin, which is inserted in its head.

We can compare ourselves with it. Our attention is like its fin. It is concentrated consciousness. Attention is a keen awareness of a particular aspect of reality. It is a segment of all information that we choose to take in and discard everything else.

We are as violent and dangerous as an anglerfish. We live in the same sea of darkness in which our attention creates an illuminated path. It helps us in catching information which is vital for survival.

We are losing the brightness of this focused attention. We are losing our attention span. We are now like an angler fish with a very low battery.

**Human angler fish**

Let's delve into the whereabouts of this superpower in this little book.

# FABLE 1



## Hedgehog and the Snake

Once there was a snake. It was very smart and lived in a small hole on its own. It had survived many winters and was likely to survive this one also. One day, there was a knock on the door.

It was a hedgehog.

"Hi, friend. Can I share your place to live during this winter?"

"Yes," said the snake.

Soon afterwards, the snake realised its mistakes. Needles in the fur of the hedgehog started to hurt him whenever he moved.

"Leave my place," said the snake.

Hedgehog curled himself into an invincible ball and said, "Whoever is not content in the place should leave."

This story gives a lesson. It tells about our situation in relation to modern technologies. All technologies are bundled inside a technology called smartphone, which is powered by another technology called the internet. And now these technologies are becoming smarter and more autonomous with every passing day.

This technological tsunami has entered our lives slowly and turned from being a utility to a necessity. We cannot eliminate it. We can tame it and use it with acceptable harm.

We have to tame this hedgehog that has entered our lives.

This book is about learning how to nurse our attention span when we have a dangerous guest in our lives. No member of the family is spared, and now these technologies are getting more intelligent day by day.

# PART 1

# CHAPTER 1

# A DISTRACTED ANIMAL

**"You are just a tiny wisp of air,
Carrying a big corpse." – Epictetus**

Humans are strange creatures. We are made up of the same stuff as everything is made up of, but still, we behave in entirely different ways when it comes to spending our time. In the good old times, when a celestial body had just obliterated the herd of dinosaurs, the main focus of humans was food and the shadow that could kill them. All attention when man was not sleeping was divided between two things.

Eat, survive, and do it again. In between, try to replicate if possible. There was never a time when he was short of attention.

Then came the sciences. The thing they do in labs with beakers and computers resembles the activities of a highly curious, paranoid, always sniffing mammal. It whacked the discomfort out of everything. There were burgers in every corner and water in every tap. For the first time in the history of the universe, there was so much free time to spend when there were no lions waiting on the next corner of your street!

Few started playing games. Few started reading alphabets which were put over flattened trees. Few drowned their brains in chemicals prepared in labs or breweries. But still, things were not getting easier.

Humans always had information around them. It was always constant. A continuous shower of irrelevant inputs falls on their senses.

When one human with a curly moustache (Einstein) discovered that space and energy were the same thing called **space-time**, other humans who never understood the complex calculations of his theory of relativity poured awards and quotes onto this scientist. Einstein said everything we observe lies in the fabric of space-time. What you mistake as gravity is a bend in this fabric of space-time.

These are like coordinates of an event in the universe. A way to locate a particular event in the whole universe: space and time.

**Boltzmann** was a cute and intelligent scientist who was taken back by God through his own hands when he committed suicide. He laid the background for the thermodynamic theory of time. It proved that entropy always increases, and this decides the arrow of time.

This arrow is always from past to future unless you are a science fiction writer.

So, whatever happens can be located on a map of the universe by its space-time tag. Two more things are required to complete the story.

One is **information**. It is everywhere. If there is no information, we will never detect it with our senses. Information is all the signals around us which alter receptors of our senses and hence change the content of our consciousness. Information is organised energy.

Then the fourth part is an **observer**. If there is no observer for this space-time and information, then it is irrelevant if they exist like we are not concerned with what lies beyond the edges of the observable universe.

So if something happens in the universe, then it needs space, time, information, and an observer to make sense of it. We can also say that space and time are also forms of information. So we are left with information and an observer.

So, space-time remained the same, with the expanding universe speeding up in all directions. The observer became more intelligent with time due to the effect of the organised information and evolution. The amount of organised information has increased with each decade in recent times. Information has become more and more organised.

It changed with time in its form but roughly human senses take in 11 million bits of data every second. Out of these, we can process 40 bits of data. And we can keep four bits of data in our working memory. So there is a mismatch. A sea of information is hitting the small receptor.

So, as a wise human being once discovered, 90 percent of everything is useless. Information feeds on attention. The more information at a point in space-time, the less free attention there is.

So we get a lot of information flooding our consciousness, but we have to choose what we need. This is called **focus**. This is what we are trying to reclaim. Throughout the generations, there have been things that feed on attention.

As time progressed, we developed new sources of information: television, radio, pop stars, gossip, newspapers, and then screens with the internet. This created an unlimited supply of information that was available with a jerk of our finger.

This was the start of the decline. A thing which was devised to save time finally killed it. As a wise man said, "When we create a ship, we also create shipwreck."

There was a shortage of one of the most abundant resources that humans had. For the first time, there was a shortage of attention.

An increase in data and its widespread availability led to the dissolution of society's hierarchy.

Now there are no privileged secrets and everyone starts from the same podium with respect to available information. All the intestines of every system and business are laid out on the internet.

An expert has 50,000 chunks of information in a particular field. Everyone has that available on demand in their pockets due to the internet.

Hence, our attention is now data-burdened and fragile due to a mismatch between the need for data and its supply.

This book is written by a man who has all the problems with his attention. He is frustrated beyond imagination by the constant poking of his focus by incoming waves of information and the disobedience of his reptilian mind towards his small prefrontal cortex.

The book has scribbles from his research to find ways to regain his focus. He waded through many books on focus to find hidden focus somewhere.

I hope someday he will be able to work for some time as Cal Newport imagined in his book *Deep Work* or the most cited author in amateur non-fiction books, Cheek-Sent-Me-High (Mihaly Csikszentmihalyi) who wrote a book about flow.

Let's try to find out if we can still retain and regain our focus.

# CHAPTER 2
# LET'S SEE WHAT IT IS

**"I succeeded because I have a long attention span."**
**– Charlie Munger**

Attention is not the same as focus. It is its big brother. It means the ability to process certain information while leaving out the rest.

Focus is attention with a certain control over it. It is the concentration of mental effort on a certain specific aspect of available information.

We are concerned with both. We want to reclaim our focus and preserve our attention span from this organised assault by information.

Everything is information. It is a bold claim, but it might be true. Everything is organised information, and it includes energy, consciousness, space, entropy, and the arrow of time. Energy is a form of mass.

Information is everywhere around an observer. If there is no observer, then we cannot decipher the information. When there is no observer, information still exists, but we are not concerned with it. We will then be hanging in oblivion, unaware of anything.

**Attention and you**

Information feeds on attention. The more information there is, the less attention is left.

**Information feeds on attention**

Attention can be imagined as a sort of flashlight from the consciousness. Although there is a big background of subconscious information, attention is mainly a creature of consciousness.

Let's see the human brain. It is a squashy mess. It has boiled our beautiful earth, but that is a topic for a different book. It rests in the dungeon of a bony skull.

It lives in such a strong barrack that our liver and kidneys feel like they are wrapped in a cloth and can be punctured by any trivial injury. Any disgruntled human driver on the road you pass every day can split open your intestines if your brain misbehaves with him by overtaking his car.

The brain has senses. These are like antennae to catch information. It has different sensors in the form of eyes, ears, skin, nose, and position sense, which is called proprioception. There are various minor senses like a sense of doom, a sense of something missing, a sense of a hole in the heart, butterflies, etc. But for our book, we can club these all into one single antenna, which sends a coherent story about things that are happening around us to our brain.

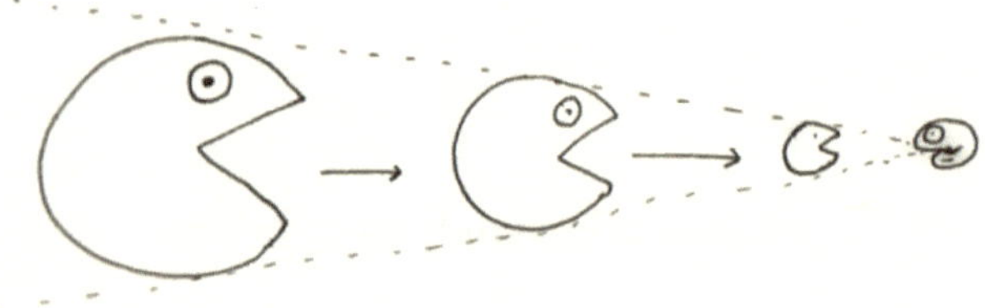

**Information feeds on attention**

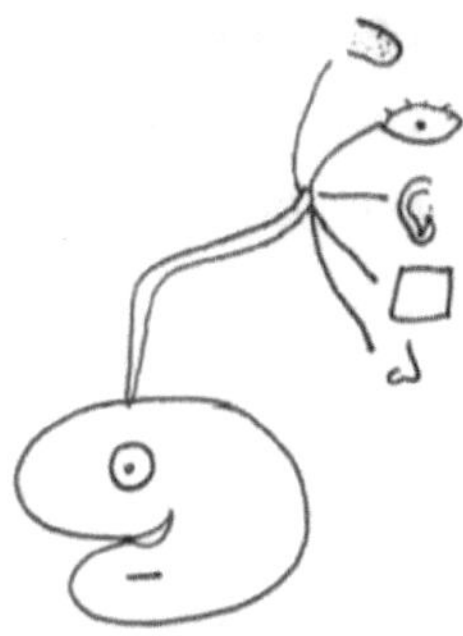

**Senses**

So our attention is sort of focusing on our senses on a particular aspect of all the information available at a point of space-time.

This can be compared to a round sphere around our brain. Our brain is like a small dot submerged in the sea of information.

Of all the information falling on us, we imbibe a little fraction. According to scientists, every second, 11 million bits of information hit us. Out of these, we can absorb 40 bits, and out of this, we can process only four bits. So we drown in a sea and drink in atoms. (Sorry for repeating this information, but I am checking to see if you are still attentive.)

We can look at our attention in this way.

**Inward focus** is looking at our inner world, which includes all the thoughts, emotions, and gut feelings. It is always on.

Then there is **Outward focus** which focuses on external stimuli. Its main purpose is to keep us safe and surviving. But currently, it is utilised to absorb reels and TikTok videos.

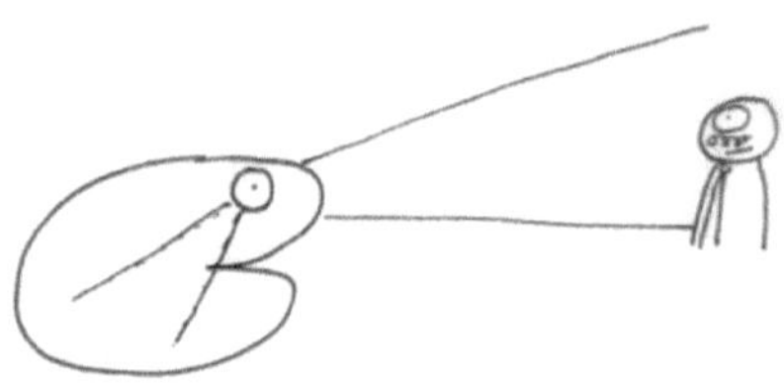

**Outward focus and inward focus**

Then there is a part of outer focus which includes other conscious beings, including animals and humans. This helps in empathy and cooperation. It is a part of our outer focus, but it is what matters a lot. You must note that your kid is slowly drifting into the same hole of overstimulation you entered last year.

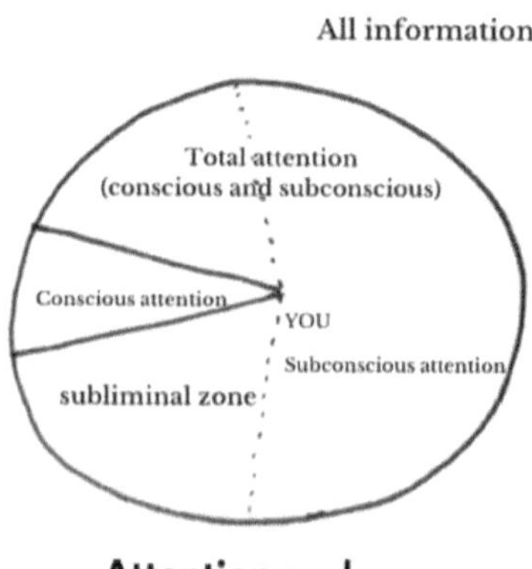


**Attention and you**

Another way to look at things is by top-down or bottom-up route.

## TYPE 1 FOCUS

Type 1 focus includes stimuli that arrive at us and enter our subconscious before reaching consciousness. This depends more on our reptile brain than on our frontal cortex, which lies behind our forehead bone.

When a picture of green veggies you do not like makes you gag, it includes a down-up focus. It warns you when you see altered geography of the face of your partner who has not uttered any fresh complaint yet.

It is fast, automatic, and always on. It helps in making habits and saving energy. It generally overpowers top-down focus after some time. It is captured by supernormal stimuli. You cannot miss a loud sound or an angry face in the crowd. You cannot miss somebody calling your name in a crowd of intoxicated humans at a cocktail party.

Then there is top-down attention. I call it **type 2 focus** by imitating the great scientist Daniel Kahneman. It is directed by our prefrontal cortex and involves the expenditure of energy.

When you open your book and manage to read as your dad circles like a violent beast around you, it is a top-down focus. It is also used to spend endless hours in your classroom. Top-down focus is slow, effortful, voluntary, and useful for self-control. It helps in making choices, doing deep work, and concentrating. It is useful after you have chosen to work on something voluntarily.

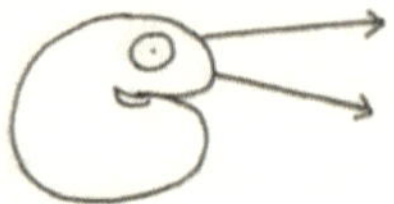

**Type 2 focus
Voluntary**

**Type 1 focus
Automatic**

This is not all. We can see attention from different angles.

Attention can be seen from this perspective, too. This is described by the great journalist **Johann Hari** in his excellent book on attention called Stolen Focus.

**Spotlight** is focused attention on one task, like reading a poem in the morning assembly.

**Starlight is** focused on long-term goals. Starlight helps you plan for retirement.

**Daylight** is focused on self-awareness.

**The stadium light** is used to see the collective goal of the team and society.

So we can summarise it like this. All information surrounds us. What enters our consciousness is awareness. It includes both conscious and subconscious data. The part of it that we retain while ignoring the rest is attention. The attention that is placed on a specific aspect of a task or observation is called focus.

Attention is the concentration of awareness in one place. The duration for which we can sustain productive or useful attention is **attention span**.

It has been reduced greatly due to the overuse of screens.

And it is not like this that a part of awareness is diverted to that spot like a piece of pizza.

It is like a light that fades as distance increases from the central focus. However, the energy of awareness is maximum in the area of focus and barely present in other parts of awareness.

This leads to **inattention blindness**. When we are too focused on a particular part of awareness or information, we are almost blind to other aspects of it. You could drive your truck into other cars if a particular reel is too cool and engaging and unusually long.

Now, let's take a different look at it again.

When we look at a thing, it provides us information about what possible action this individual or animal can take. This is called **affordance**. It is a bunch of actions that the living beings can do depending on their intelligence. When we see a chubby baby in the crowd, we see his chubby cheeks. Our hands tingle to pinch the baby to make him smile.

Then there is a point or specific place of the object where action can happen called **signifier**. The dimple in the baby's cheek is a **signifier**.

Our attention always segregates affordances and signifiers from the surroundings.

Hush. Are you still there?

# PART 2

# CHAPTER 3

# BONES AND BATTERIES OF ATTENTION

**"Attention is the rarest and purest form of generosity."**
**– Simone Weil**

Reality is odourless and colourless. We use our senses to create models of reality, which include smells, colours, and textures. These create rough models of reality that help us to respond to our surroundings.

When we see our brain, there are layers like an onion in it. First, there is general intelligence. It has many components like senses, short-term memory, long-term memory, fluid intelligence, and static intelligence.

Although scientists are not sure about how attention works, we still have many theories to explain this.

Attention has many parts.

First is its **direction.** It can be in the present, past, or even future. We are concerned with the present focus in this book. Focus on the past and future are parts of systems involved in creativity, imagination, and reflection.

Another aspect is the duration of attention. It is very important as it determines the productivity in any particular work. The higher the duration of quality attention, the higher the quality of the work done. It may not increase creativity, but the craft phase improves with the length of the span.

With time, the attention span of humans is falling under the carpet. It is barely noticeable. A cat can win an attention span bout with an average human.

Another aspect is the depth of focus. Superficial focus is common. Sometimes one is giving partial attention to more than one task. This is called **continuous partial attention.**

When you are playing Minecraft and your father is trying to transfer his life wisdom to your brain, then you sometimes practice this. This is like a faint light one puts on a thing he does not want to see. It is getting common in human civilisation, especially among younger ones.

**Continuous partial attention**

**Deep focus** is when a person is deeply focused on a particular meaningful work that is aligned with their long-term goals.

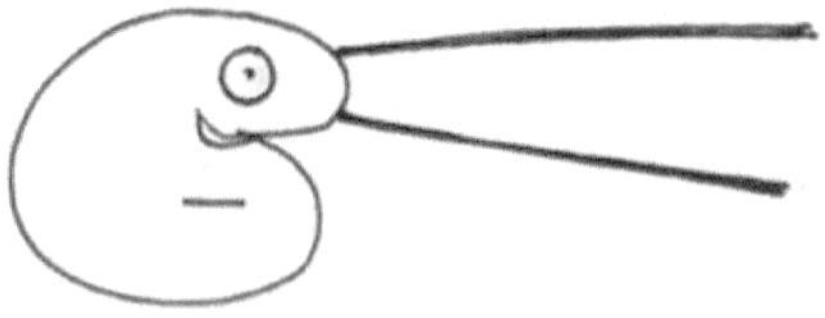

## Deep focus

Attention can be **overt** when we can track it and observe it. It can be done by tracking the eyes of a person when he reads a book. A group of monks sitting by the side of a mountain can be easily monitored for the level of their attention.

The second type of attention is **covert.** It is not visible to the observer. It is the skill that you use to pick up the phone of your mother when she moves from her position as a guard, even for a few microseconds. She never knows that you are watching over her phone like a hungry hound.

It can be **sustained attention** when you stare at the waiter who has served ice cream to all the kids, leaving you in between. Sustained attention needs energy, and it falls after 20 minutes. Hence, attention needs energy, like all meaningful things in life.

It can be **selective attention** when you eat your plate of noodles while a hungry beggar looks inside from the window.

It can be an **alternate focus** when you watch a tennis match in the stadium or when you see two fighting humans who speak loudly in turns.

**Shared attention** is when two humans or animals have focus on a common object and can understand the intentions of each other. Shared attention is also of different types.

It can be a **simply shared gaze** in which two humans look at the same object or person, like humans watching a pop star in a concert as he blows out their eardrums.

It can **dyadic** attention shared attention in which they converse alternately with gestures. It happens between human adults and infants who slowly learn all the bad habits from the human adults.

Then, there is **triadic attention,** which is the highest sort of attention. Two forward footballers share such deep attention and know each other's intention to score a goal in a football match. Also, between the two lovers, as they walk in the crowd.

Then there is arousal level in attention. If we are like a **sloth** in our arousal, we hardly do anything even if trying deep focus. A lover in a fit of extreme love can accomplish superhuman tasks, such as cleaning his room after 13 months, as his girlfriend might visit that day.

Performance is not linearly related to arousal level. As arousal level increases, performance increases up to a certain extent and then it falls. It is called **Yerkes-Dodson curve.**

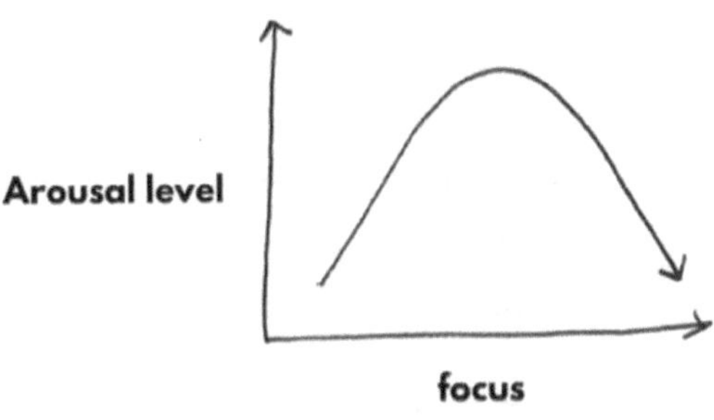



**Arousal and focus**

The next aspect of attention is its target. It can be **goal-directed,** like focusing on the chips of a packet in the hands of your sibling.

Or it can be without a particular target. It is called **open awareness or mind-wandering.** It is the source of human creativity and insights. It can be thought of as a focus on our subconscious, which then provides us with useful things. All the jewels and scorpions are hidden deep in our subconscious.

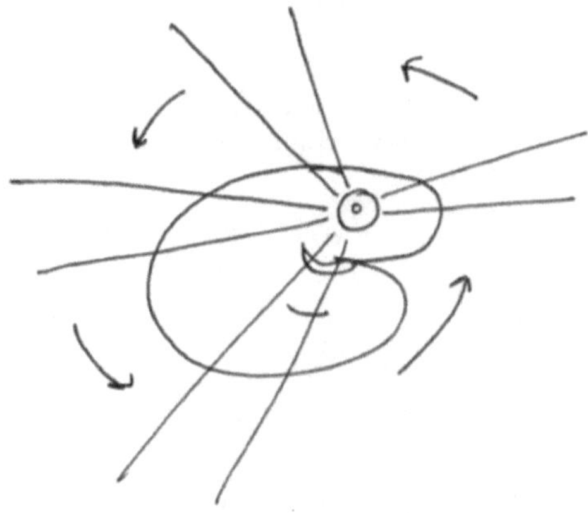

**Mind wandering**

## What is inside?

The next aspect is the **content** of the attention. It can be sensation, memory, thought, urge, habit, or any combination of these. It can be filled with multiple tasks or rarely with one task.

Now, let's try to simplify attention and focus so that we can understand them better.

This is a human brain, and this dot represents its centre. It is enveloped in information from all directions. Then, there is a small segment of awareness which comes to consciousness. It is attention. When directed to a particular aspect of information, it is called focus. It is like a small cone that starts from the brain and extends to the extreme reaches of awareness. This limit depends on the sensitivity of our senses. Without technology, this reach is not very far.

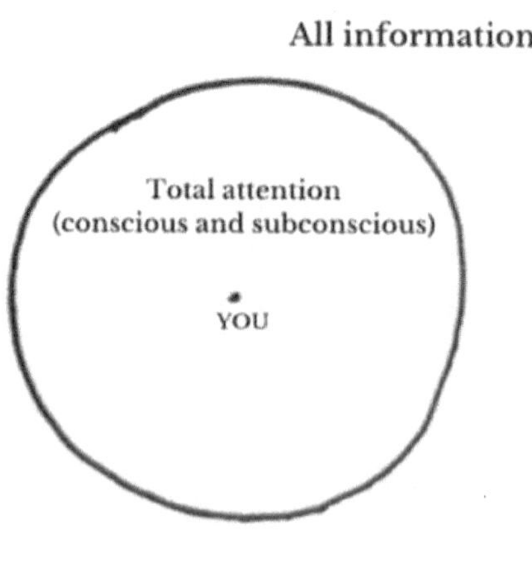


**Attention and you**

Part outside this conscious cone is our subconscious awareness. And everything outside of this is information to which we are blind at that particular moment.

Also, we should know that the form of information also matters. The medium of information matters. Sound frequencies above or below our hearing range are missing from our awareness and hence from our attention.

There are other ways to see our attention that I have still not mentioned here. Let's see them.

Attention is of three types if we classify it based on utility.

The first is **orienting attention.** This makes us aware of a change in the environment. If there is a change in the current model of a scene, then it updates the change and creates a new model for that moment.

It is called **focal attention** if it is targeted at a particular object or space or background in full intensity. It can be a single focus or a divided focus on more than one stimulus.

The second type is **filtering attention.** It filters the multiple inputs to report the relevant and important information to our brain. It helps you to pick up especially buttery and sugary packets of food on the endless shelves of a supermarket.

The third type of attention is **searching attention,** in which we scan a large area to find the target thing or place.

It can be controlled or automatic. Automatic takes less effort. It can be an easy search or a difficult search depending on the context and the amount of information and its organisation.

Next let's learn how science treats attention and focus.

# CHAPTER 4

# LAB COAT WEARING SCIENTISTS AND ATTENTION

**"Tell me what you pay attention to, and I will tell you who you are." – Jose Gasset**

There are three parts to an event of focus.

First is the observer. Then, there is attention or focus. Third is the source of information. We shall study every part in brief.

The brain is a collection of electrical currents produced by chemicals in water and fat coverings. It has various parts.

When the brain is not active, it is still very active. This was a strange discovery by scientists. This is called the **default mode network.** It is the network activated when we are not doing any task. It disappears as soon as you start to focus.

It uses 20% of the total energy at rest. This network is thought to be very important for creativity and insights. It is localised in the medial part of the prefrontal cortex and cingulate gyrus. It is associated with autobiographical memory (me, self-reference, emotional regulation, and social and moral decisions).

Self-awareness has two parts:

The first part is 'Me', which includes past and future memories.

The second part is 'I', which is concerned with the present state.

**David Bernyle,** in his book *Search after Truth*, was the first to state that attention is necessary to organise ideas.

The brain has the memory to remember things on which it has attention. This is working memory, which is used for focusing attention. For storage, there is short-term memory and long-term memory, but these come later on.

Attention space is limited and finite. It can be increased by meditation and practice. Working memory holds the information before transferring it to short-term memory.

Attention space can hold one complex task in it, or it can hold one habit and a medium difficulty level task. In multitasking, it holds multiple inputs.

Short-term memory is around 18-20 seconds, and it is highly volatile. According to **Ebbinghaus,** we forget memories at a very fast pace.

He was a German psychologist who studied memory. He discovered the forgetting curve and the value of spacing to increase learning and retention. He showed that we lose information quickly over time.

At one time, we can remember seven plus or minus two chunks of information.

Chunks are grouping of data into specific groups for easy retrieval. Like 123321123321123321 can be remembered as chunks of 123 and reversed 321. This chunk theory was given by **George A. Miller.** He was an American psychologist who liked to do research and play golf. He lived a productive life and died due to complications of pneumonia at the age of 92 years.

**Our working memory is limited**

So the brain filters information to catch only the relevant parts due to its limited capacity. It is called **bottleneck theory or filter theory.** It was given by **Wundt,** who is considered the father of attention theory. William Wundt was a German philosopher who was a pioneer in experimental psychology, and he did excellent work throughout his life before his peaceful death at the age of 88 years.

**Unorganized information**

We get information. We filter out the useful and integrate it into short-term memory. It is called **apperception.** This term was given by **Leibniz.** It creates a new whole by mixing two memories – old and new ones.

Leibniz was a German polymath who has many institutions named after him. He never married and near his death, he was out of reputation in the eyes of the king and his scientific association. His funeral was not attended by crowds, and his grave remained unmarked for 50 years. This shows that universe can be cruel sometimes.

**Helmholtz** discovered that attention is necessary for visual processing. What we see needs our attention to enter into our awareness clearly.

Then information can be processed early or late during the processing of the information.

According to Donald **Broadbent,** information is filtered early in processing, and hence, after that point, only filtered information goes further. All chaos is filtered out early, and only relevant parts are let in so that things do not get messed up in the later part. Broadbent was a scientist from the United Kingdom who proposed the filter theory of attention.

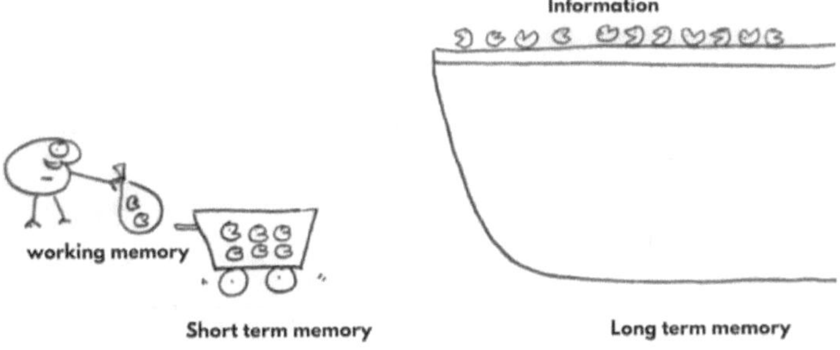


**Treisman** said that an unattended stimulus is attenuated while taking in the data. **Treisman** was the brain behind feature integration theory. She divorced her husband and married the legendary Nobel Prize-winning **scientist Daniel Kahneman.**

She found that in early processing, the visual system encodes various features like shape, contour, and colour in different maps which are then integrated to create the reality of the scene. If there is any interference with early encoding, then there are errors in the observation. We may mistake a clay piece that our toddler left on the floor for a lizard.

But this does not explain **cocktail party effect.** When you are at a party and someone speaks your name, it immediately enters your awareness, even if you are not attending to it. This cocktail party effect goes against the early processing theory. It goes straight into the consciousness. Who the hell is talking about me! You think.

Another theory is **spotlight theory,** in which attention falls on a specific place like a spotlight. However, it does not explain how we can separately focus on two superimposed pictures at the same place, as in a puzzle.

So focus is more dynamic and flexible. It changes according to circumstances to provide the best response to information. This resulted in the formulation of the **theory of integrated competition.**

## Time stamp of attention

Along with the content of attention, there is also time perception in each act of focus. In our mind, a shorter interval is overestimated, and a longer one is underestimated. It is called **Vierodt's effect.**

If in a stimulus there are breaks or frequent changes or if it is louder, then time is perceived as longer.

If an observer is motivated, time runs faster.

When we are in awe due to any event, time slows down due to deep processing. The same happens in an acute, severe, frightening event like a situation in which you find something crawling on your back.

If a novel stimulus is presented to the brain, then its perceived time is longer. It is called **oddball effect.** The same happens with deviant or surprising stimuli.

As we age, time runs faster due to a more habitual life. So we can say that apart from the more automatic life, older humans are happy after surviving the long-term thrashing given by life.

Then there is the phenomenon of **chronostasis** which we have observed firsthand ourselves. A YouTube music video is slower when watched the first time and then it speeds up when we watch it again after it ends as the brain filters out non-relevant details.

The brain also adapts itself to accommodate the thing of its focus. If you are a cab driver in London and it has been a while, then the part of your brain involved in remembering maps and roads will be bigger.

Similarly, if you play the violin to pay your bills, then the part of your brain trained to pull the right chords becomes bulky. This is called **omega sign.**

But how attention feeds on information is an interesting story that you must know.

# CHAPTER 5

# HOW ATTENTION EATS ITS FOOD

**"A successful warrior is the average man with laser focus." – Bruce Lee**

**P**erception is the entering of information into attention and **apperception** is the entry into inner memory.

When we get any information, we process it as a whole, which is created by combining small components of the information.

Knowledge is appreciated as a whole, not in bits. This is **Gestalt psychology.** Hence, the sum of small ideas is larger than the sum of individual components.

Sensations are finite when you are watching a silent horizon but infinite if you are scrolling on Google. The infinite scroll function of the internet never ends, and you can keep scrolling forever if you pay your bills on time.

Current social media is negatively biased and switches information rapidly, learning along the way about ways to stimulate your primal desires and fears. It learns your habits and serves you exactly what you like. There is no escape from this trap.

The brain is hardwired to do a few tricks to make sense of the surroundings.

**Reification** is the process by which the brain receives more explicit information than the sensory input available. For example, we create illusory contours in the following diagram.

**Law of closure**

**Reification - More interpretation from less information**

**Multistability** is the ability to process the same information in two mutually exclusive forms. This phenomenon is observed when viewing **Necker's cube and Rubin's vase. (Google them, but don't get lost in an endless scroll of information!)**

Also, we group the sensory inputs into meaningful formations. Sensory inputs lying close to each other are grouped into separate heaps.

There is the **law of proximity** in which sensations that are close to each other are taken as a group.

**Law of proximity**

There is the **law of similarity** in which two similar stimuli are taken to be a part of one group.

**Law of similarity**

We seek closure of the sensory input sequence. We fill in the gaps to complete the story.

We can fill gaps in live playing of information. We have a **blind spot** in each of our eyes. There are no nerves in the area, but still, we create the complete picture of whatever we see. So there is a lot of editing going on.

So, our attention gets an edited version of reality due to our senses and brain, which helps reduce confusion.

But our attention is also fragile. It can falter, and this happens frequently.

Information can get lost. It can get lost in space as well as it can get lost in time.

There is one clever experiment in psychology. Experimenters asked passersby to give directions to a place. In between two actors, with a wooden gate crossed, the person asking questions was replaced by another person. Fifty percent of people could not notice the change. This is **change blindness.** Changing a non-peculiar thing or a thing of less interest in the same setting can be missed. So you need to be weird to be picked up by human attention if you are surrounded by similar people.

Then there is **attention blinking,** which is different from an eye blink. If we send two stimuli to the eyes in quick succession and ask the person what he saw, if the second one is very close to the first thing noticed, then it can be missed by attention, which is still processing the last thing. This shows a bottleneck in the speed of sensory processing.

We cannot process all stimuli, and we cannot process stimuli quickly.

This limit is exploited by the magicians and movie editors.

One strange phenomenon is **repetition blindness.** If we present our attention with the same stimuli in quick succession, then the brain may not process the repeated stimuli again and keeps the last stimuli in its processing system and working memory.

This is the reason behind the problem of divided attention. More than one stimulus interferes with each other. The way in which stimuli are presented decides the amount of mental effort required to process them.

Attention is divided. This is the reason why the same information given through two sensory organs reduces performance. This is called the **redundancy effect.** If you are shown a picture of Taylor Swift with eye, ear, legs, brain, back, and hair labels on the picture, it can get quite disconcerting for her fans.

But our brains read words as a whole and not individual letters to make meaning of text. Due to this, you can read the lines even if words are jumbled or even mixed with mathematical numbers.

**"This is bcuseae the huamn mind**

**Deos not raed ervey lteter**

**By istlef, but the word as a wlohe,"**

You can easily read both the forms of this sentence. Correct sentence is as below.

"This is because the human mind does not read every letter by itself, but the word as a whole."

One strange phenomenon is **extinction.** When a less important stimulus is present continuously, then we may ignore it. Like a scratch on our spectacles or floaters in our eye, which are not visible routinely. We see them if we try to focus on these. But they do not intrude on our attention unnecessarily.

Also, there is the **Stroop effect,** which shows that irrelevant stimuli reduce our performance. In it, various colours are written on a page, and the colour of the fonts used is not the same as the colour name. This reduces the identification and processing of this information.

The same interference is behind the increased chances of banging into the next vehicle on the road if we are texting while driving.

Patients in whose brains blood clots form get damage to particular areas of their brain.

If the right parietal cortex is damaged, then the patient neglects the information from the left half of the body. This is called **hemi-neglect.** This was beautifully illustrated in the book, "The Man Who Mistook His Wife for a Hat." In it, a woman in her sixties forgets to notice food on the left side of her plate due to hemi-neglect.

In a more severe version where both sides of the Prieto-occipital areas of the brain are damaged, there is **bilateral** neglect. It creates **Bliant syndrome.** A person can detect only one object at a time, and even if two balls are lying side by side, he will see only one.

When we are too focused on one thing, attention is absent for all other stimuli. This is the cause of inattention blindness. Even if a gorilla dances in the background or your mum is ready with her slap when you are watching TV for two hours with the same piece of food in your mouth. This is very dangerous. People can die taking selfies, and sportsmen could collide when they give all their attention to one ball they have to catch.

The memory champions we respect are actually focus champions. They create frameworks in mind over which they hang data and retrieve it. It is all about focus and does not involve cramming things.

There are few things that kill attention and we cannot move ahead without knowing about them.

# CHAPTER 6
# SOURCES OF ANTI ATTENTION

**"Simplicity means focused attention."**
**– Edward de Bono**

## Source of Anti-attention

Then there is the source. It can be anything we see.

It can be a silent scene of a winter forest that gives information that it will be better to pull our legs inside the gates. It can be light or sound or smell or a change in pressures. It can be an internal signal from the graveyard of memories. It can be a piece of imagination stuck somewhere in the brain.

We can process 1% of the visual data available to us at any given instant. Attention can be internal or external. Data can overload your attention.

**Cognitive overload** makes you process more information than your capacity, and **perceptual overload** happens when the number of stimuli is huge.

Stimuli can fool our senses as evolution has made our brain just good enough but not perfect. So it is very easily fooled by stimuli which escape our fixed patterns. Things that our eye stamps as being hyper-authentic could just be a glitch in the interpretation system.

## Muller's lines

These two lines are equal but our brain tells us otherwise.

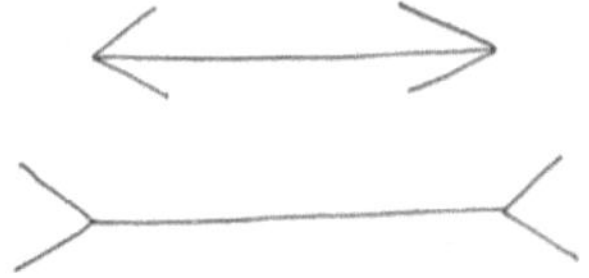

Muller Lyer illusion

## Zollners illusion

These lines are parallel but our brain tells us otherwise.

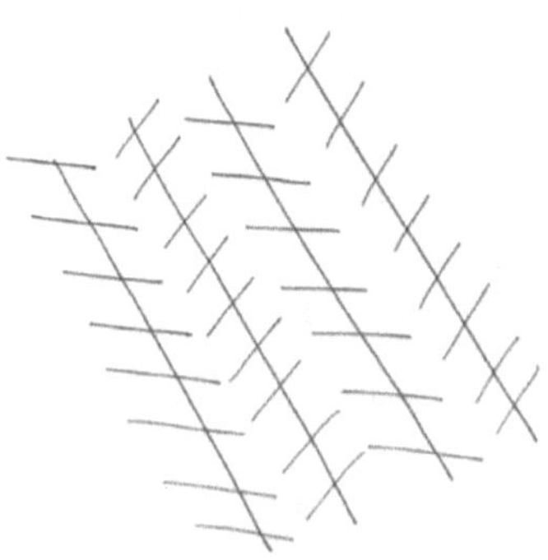

Zollner illusion

Even stimuli that are below the perception threshold due to low intensity or rapid disappearance can enter attention. These are called **subliminal stimuli.**

Body language experts rely on these subliminal signals to catch the possible serial killer or a lying crook. Also, one should be aware of the fact that words convey only 10% of information; the rest is given by tone of voice and body language.

The direction from which stimuli come is also relevant. You are a symmetrical animal, but not perfect. Stimuli on the same side of the response have better performance than when both stimulus and response are on opposite sides. This is called the **Simon effect.**

When two people see the same event, they create different stories and narratives due to differences in their perception. This is called the **Rashomon effect.** This shows that we live in different realities. Along with input and its processing, the difference in focus creates different realities.

This effect was named after the 1950 Japanese movie called Rashomon in which different characters give different accounts of how a samurai had died.

This was studied by German scientist **Jacob Uwexkul,** who described that every life form lives in its own unique reality due to differences in senses, perceptions, and brain processing.

A human sitting on his sofa with a cat by his side, a rat behind the sofa, and a bee sitting on his TV screen all see different realities. These are called **Umwelt** in the German language.

There are a few stimuli that are sticky. **Earworms** are auditory stimuli that enter the brain through the ears and are hard to get rid of. Even in discomfort, we keep singing the tone for a long time.

**Pareidolia** is a distinctly human trait, especially in empathetic individuals. In it, we see meaning in irrelevant information. A devoted man can see Jesus in the toast, snakes in the clouds, or faces in toilet taps. A tree at night can appear as a bear.

In some situations, sensations may be felt in the absence of the source. **Phantom limb syndrome** makes the person feel the pain from an amputated limb.

**Silas Wer Mitchell** was a doctor who published a case of **George Deadlow** in 1866 in the Atlantic Monthly. He had amputated a limb but still felt sensations in it: itch, stretch, bend, a feeling of being wet, and pain. A large number of amputees experience this sensation, which captures our attention without a visible source.

Then there is the ever-present fake news, which travels six times faster than the truth.

Focus is a superpower. Memory champions are not actually memory champions but champions of focus. They arrange information in discrete patterns by deep focus and practice.

Magicians also use your focus to their advantage. They focus your brain on a place where the event is not happening and then dazzle you. Once you know how the trick is being done, you cannot unsee it, and it fails to surprise you.

# CHAPTER 7

# SUBTYPES OF ATTENTION AND ITS INTERACTIONS

**"Success is the ability to focus well."**
**– Jack Canfield**

Now, let's explore the depths and subtypes of our attention.

We can divide stimuli into a matrix based on two factors.

First, if we have control over it, and second, if it is distracting or not for us.

If we have control and it's disturbing, then it can be our phone, trading app, or Candy Crush Saga.

If we have control and it is not a distraction, then it could be deep focus.

Things over which we have no control and are distracting are visitors and construction work nearby.

Things over which we have no control and are still not distracting are mild background noises and mild discomfort in our back.

Divide your distractions based on it and control things on which you have control. Adapt to or accept the rest.

Another way to see your attention is in this way.

The first factor is whether it is productive for us to focus on, and the second is its entertainment value.

Attractive and productive work is purposeful.

Attractive and non-productive work is a distraction.

Non-attractive and unproductive work is a duty.

Harmful and unproductive work is stupidity.



**Focus and energy matrix**

Focus present     Focus absent

| | Focus present | Focus absent |
|---|---|---|
| **You have control** | Deep focus | Mind wandering |
| **No control** | Flow | Distractions |

**Focus and effort required matrix**

| | Attractive work | Non attractive work |
|---|---|---|
| **Productive work** | Flow | Duty |
| **Non productive work** | Waste | Chores |

**Attractive and productive work matrix**

# Types of distractions:

| | Not fun | Fun |
|---|---|---|
| **No control** | Meetings | Family calls |
| **control** | Notifications | Instagram |

# CHAPTER 8
# SPECIAL TYPES OF ATTENTION

**"Focus determines your reality." – George Lucas**

These are useful types of attention that we wish to achieve.

The first is **hyperfocus.** This term is usually associated with research related to attention deficit hyperactivity syndrome. It was made famous by the author Chris Bailey in his book of the same name. It is a deep focus on one productive task with our intention, which is aligned with your long-term goal. This leads to maximum productivity, especially if the task does not need creativity or innovation.

Hyperfocus is a precursor to the state of flow.

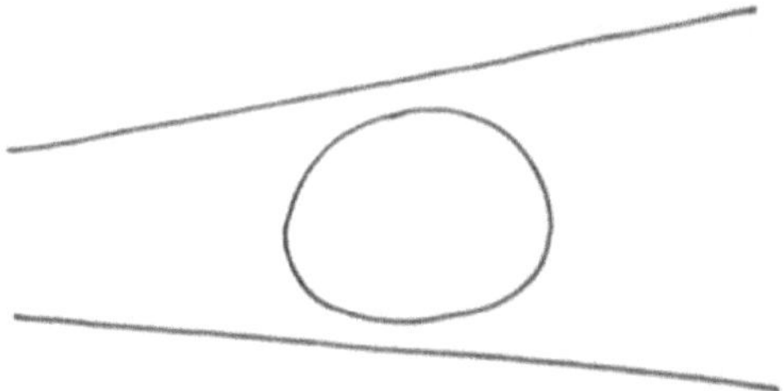

## Hyper focus

Then there is **deep focus.** It was made famous by one of my favourite professors, Cal Newport. He called it deep work. It is distraction-free concentration on a task to push your mental abilities to their limits and results in high-quality productivity.

Then there is **mind-wandering.**

It involves the default mode network. In this state, the mind is free to watch its movements without effort, or a habitual less effort requiring work is done, leaving a large space for capturing any inputs from the subconscious. This is the state for artists, scientists, and innovators. It is the state where the subconscious reveals its secrets, many of which are very useful. Boring and routine settings start mind-wandering automatically.

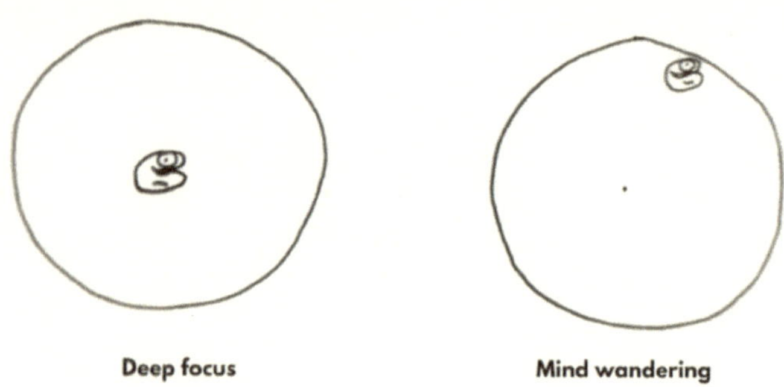



Mind-wandering can be done in different ways.

One is **capture mode** in which you capture the useful ideas out of all ideas that come into your awareness. You are not judging or trying to fetch ideas.

Another way is **problem-solving mode.** You think about a problem, keep it in the back of your mind, and sleep with it on your mind. Solutions come out suddenly many a times.

Third way to wander your mind is by doing a **habitual work** and letting your mind wander freely while doing it.

Mind-wandering is good for us. It helps us in making sense of the world as it is necessary for reflection.

What your dad said after seeing your report card needs reflection to make sense of it. It makes new connections between things you know. Hence, it provides new solutions to your problems. People have discovered the structure of benzene and the atomic table while their minds wandered in sleep.

It helps in planning for the future so that we do not end up boiling this planet above the boiling point of our bodies.

One state of focus is **flow.** It is the state where deep focus needs little effort, and perception of time is lost due to inherent enjoyment in the work. It happens when we work on a clear, meaningful work we like, and it is at the outermost capacity of our abilities.

There is also **attention from society.** Suddenly, a large number of members of the population may get focused on a particular thing, like an event or thing. This is called joint focus. This is very important. It creates viral videos, revolutions, uprisings, petitions, and paradigm changes and leads to the selection of politicians.

## Stories of a Teenager and a kid – Attention of masses

An emaciated young man lies on the bed, and his father, with a crying face in deep desperation, holds his hand to pull him out of the inevitable. Other family members watch with a mixture of fear and pain. The young man is dying a slow death.

This picture was printed on t-shirts of United Colours of Benetton. It created waves and changed the architecture of brains of the public. No one ever saw the face of AIDS, but it was the closest one could see into the eyes of this dreaded malady. This picture became the face of the HIV AIDS awareness movement.

Pictures can move masses, and this did. People and authorities became more aware of their duties.

So, public attention rises in waves and gets triggered by some discrete and peculiar information.

Even more tragic was the picture taken on the beach of the Mediterranean Sea in 2015. A two-year-old who has just lost his mother and brother to the sea lies on his stomach. His sandals are brown, and his T-shirt is red. The photographer cannot dare to check if he is breathing. No human has such courage except maybe a doctor. He just takes the picture, and when it circulates on the web, it breaks hearts. Still, I get the feeling of a sharp needle piercing my heart every time I stumble on this unbearable image. It is one of the most painful images ever taken.

It made the French President call the Turkish president and brought the refugee crisis into the world's eye. It shifted the world power centre. Two-year-old Syrian refugee boy Alan Kurdi showed the world what tragedies befall upon the unlucky.

So, certain pieces of information carry more weight and can pull the focus of a huge audience. All pictures are not the same, and some are infinitely deeper.

When we want to capture any information with our attention, then a piece of paper can act like a black hole. It absorbs data very efficiently.

# CHAPTER 9
# FOCUSING ON PAPER

**"What you focus on, expands."**

Paper is a strange thing. It can be imposing on an accomplished artist but can be fun for a little child. It is a starting station for many journeys or it can be a surface asking questions in an exam. It can be a container to eat your spicy onion and gram mix or it can be clothing to save the grace of a book. It can be a weapon to kill flies or it can be an umbrella in light rain. Paper is a versatile tool.

We can use paper to focus. It directs our attention from our eyes to our brain to our hands and then secures the content on paper. Paper is like a gym for building up attention muscle.

Not only our brain but also our hands can help us focus.

Let's discuss a few things that help to align our focus in the right direction.

## Eisenhower box

Eisenhower was a five-star army general in the US Army and then president of that nation. He is credited with this simple technique to slice through chaos and focus on important work. Work is divided based on importance and urgency.

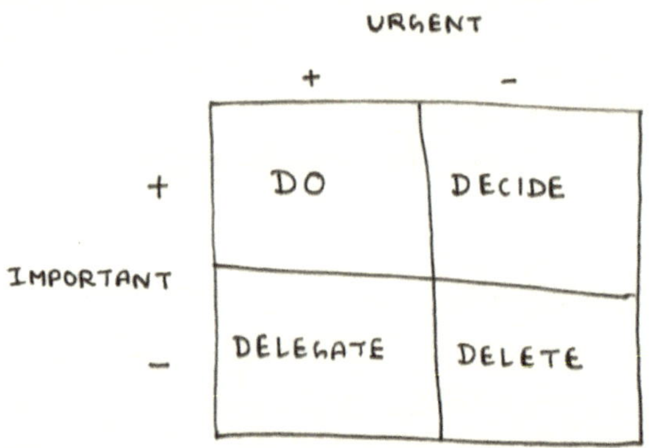


## Ivy lee method

Ivy Lee was a publicity expert from America and the founder of modern-day public relations.

Ivy Lee formulated his simple daily routine for achieving peak productivity:

At the end of each workday, write down the six most important things you need to accomplish tomorrow.

Prioritise those six items in order of their true importance.

When you arrive tomorrow, concentrate only on the first task.

Work until the first task is finished before moving on to the second task.

Approach the rest of your list in the same fashion.

At the end of the day, move any unfinished items to a new list of six tasks for the following day.

Repeat this process every working day.

## Two lists of Warren Buffett

Warren Buffett is a Coke-sipping investor with piles of cash larger than many countries. He created a way to eliminate the crap out of life.

Write down your most important 25 goals in life.

Then, circle the top 5.

Start working on these and throw away the 20 until you achieve the first five goals.

## Writing a journal

Write the truth. Write naturally and fast.

Date the entry and protect its privacy.

Reflect and investigate the core issues.

Keep it and read it again in the future.

Write every day and write for a time that you can sustain daily.

## Types of journaling

Travel Journal

Reflections

Bullet Journal

Free writing

Unsent letters

Gratitude Journal

Daily life journal

Dream Journal

Stream of consciousness journaling

TLC Journal (Thanks, Learning, Connections)

## Agile Results by J. D. Meier

Rule of 3

There are three basics.

Focus on the value of your work and not on its volume.

Focus on the outcome of your activities and not on the activity itself.

Focus on the energy available to you and not on the time spent.

## 168 Hours Concept by Laura Vanderkam

You have 168 hours available in a week. So take your time as a precious diamond and use it on things that really matter.

## Action Priority Matrix

It is used to decide which task to work on first of all.

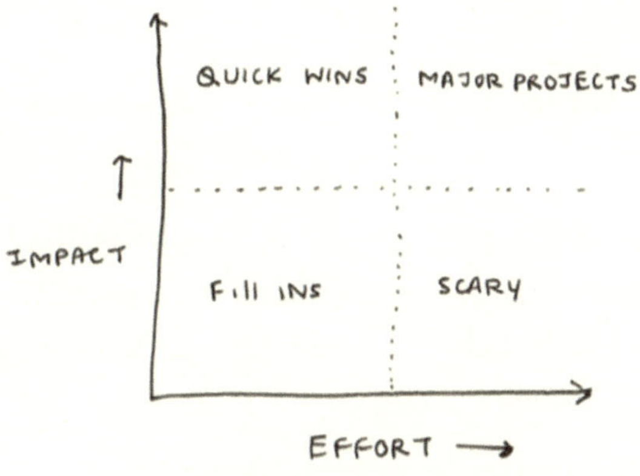


**Priority and effort matrix**

# CHAPTER 10
# SHAPE OF ATTENTION

**"It is during the darkest times that we must focus on light." – Aristotle**

Attention is like a snake painted over time. If we watch change in attention with time, it creates many wonderful curves. These curves help us make sense of our attention.

**Society's attention to new problem phases**

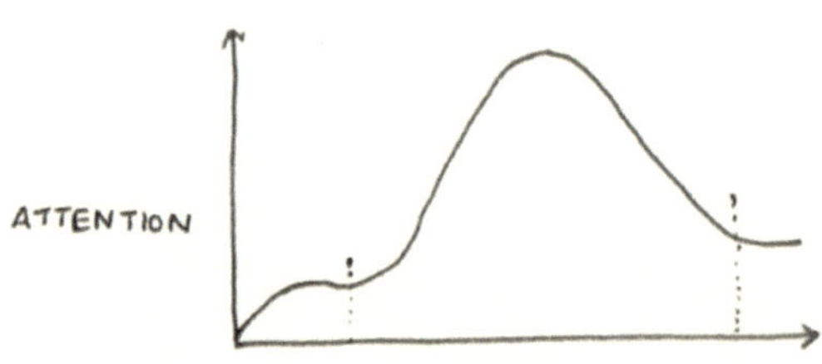



Issue life cycle curve

**A social issue and its fate**

# Lecture attention curve and Musical concert attention curve

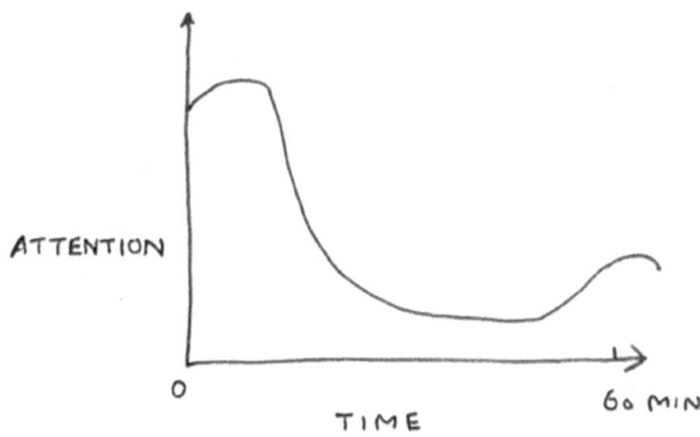



**Attention in a lecture hall**

# Gartner hype cycle

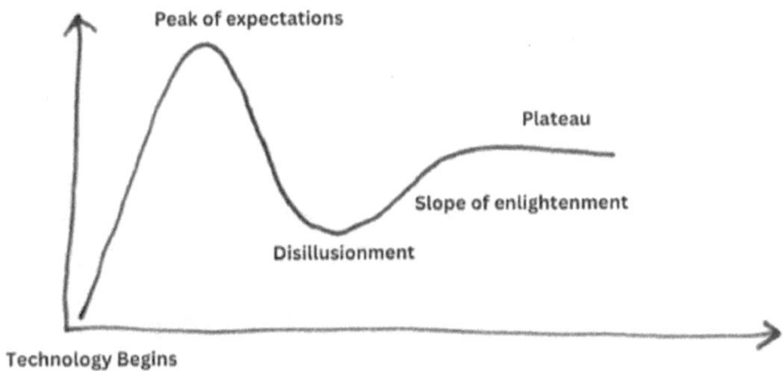



## Gartner's hype cycle for new technology

## Curve of Focus of Society on New Technology

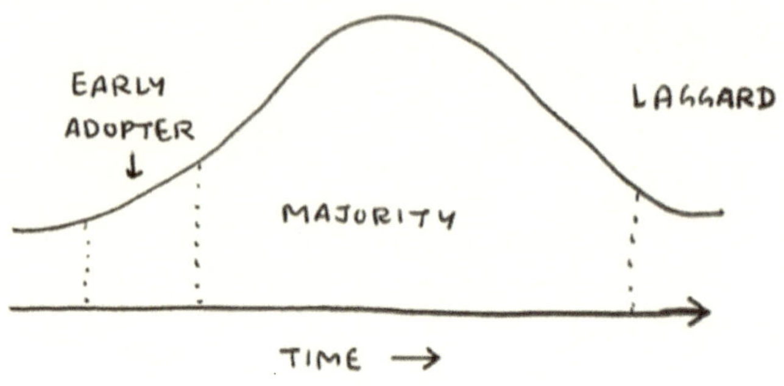


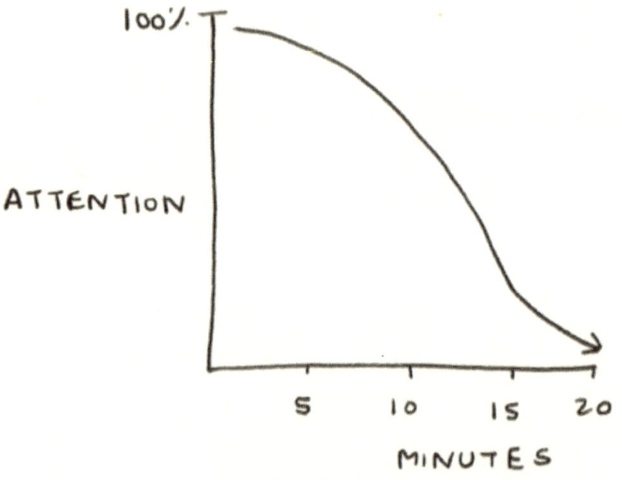


**Sustained attention curve**

## Curve of Sustained Attention

# PART 2 ½

# CHAPTER 11
# WHY THIS DAY HAS COME?

**"Where focus goes, energy flows." – Tony Robbins**

Humans are strange creatures. They can live with snakes in a glass cabin or even in a box floating in space. But they find it very hard to live with themselves. They try very hard to keep themselves amused with anything available in place of being on their own.

We love distractions. These have been constant in our history. First, there were folk songs, plays, and dances of tribal people. Then newspapers, radio, television, video games, social media, and smartphones.

We go to these to get away from the present and to get a dopamine kick by small doses of entertainment. We have become descendants of the mythological God **Tantalus.** He was continuously in search and never satisfied with whatever was presented to him.

We choose one discomfort over another. We go in pursuit of something so that we do not have to deal with what is actually there.

As **Samuel Johnson** said, "My life is a long escape from myself."

We fear pain or its milder form called discomfort. Pleasure we seek is also an effort to escape our wants to feel pleasure. So we choose our responses to alleviate this discomfort from the want of pleasure and discomforts of reality.

To resolve these issues, we choose to act, and what we usually do is a habitual, unhealthy response to this situation. It is generally harmful in the long run, but it is what we can do right now to numb the discomfort.

When there is a mismatch between the stimulation available and our expectations, then it is called **boredom.** We do not like it.

We adapt to every good feeling in some time and want more. This is a hedonic adaptation. We want to close open loops. We cannot sit still if we see an unresolved problem. We have not analysed its relevance in the long-term. We think that a comment from one stranger on Twitter should be paid back right now at 1 am, even if you will feel like a damp snail in the office tomorrow.

You want the world to function exactly as you expected; otherwise, you will become sad and do things that numb this sadness.

So, we lose our focus due to our inability to handle discomfort, reality, and uncertainty.

This is the basic layer of our failing. This is the weakness that is utilised by every hawk working on our attention.

Other smaller layers in it are **novelty bias,** in which we are attracted to a new type of stimuli, and **negativity bias,** which makes us jump and take notice of any negative stimulus like pain, loud sound, or a warning.

One such hawk feasting on our attention is **capitalism.** It is a system described by Adam Smith and exploited by shrewd businessmen. It has now turned into what is called **surveillance capitalism.** Johann Hari nicely describes this in his book *Stolen Focus.* This term was coined by American author **Shoshana Zuboff.**

There is one valley called Silicon Valley. There are intelligent people there who are experts in creating computer programs and gadgets.

They have discovered a new currency that no one could imagine had value: our attention. Now, they have come up with ever newer tricks to capture the attention of the masses. No one is spared, whether it's a kid whose teacher is waiting for his homework, a pilot who is about to fly a plane or a truck driver who is going at a speed of 100 km/h. Everyone has their attention hooked into small devices run by Silicon Valley.

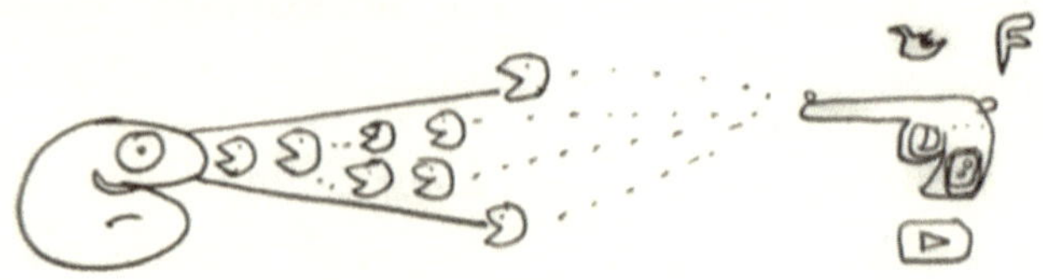

## Surveillance capitalism

They create your profile based on data you happily provide to them to register, play, earn, or receive advertisements.

They give you variable rewards and provide you with small packets of entertainment that excite your primitive instincts. They slowly collect layers of you to create a full copy of your personality. This profile keeps updating every second.

Then, they sell it in the open market. This is done by placing the right advertisement in front of the right client. To big businesses who want your attention and then your money.

This is a huge nexus. (It is also the name of the next book by Yuval Harari) on which you have very little control. They are always there once you are connected to the internet. When you ask for directions, want news, a song, or a laugh, or want to kill boredom, they note it in their digital diary.

When such big minds are working to steal your attention, then you have very little chance.

On top of that, there is a big team of people and content creators who fuel what is called **cruel optimism.** This is a mindset in which the problem is attributed to the failure of the individual who faces it.

If Zuckerberg is collecting your data and using it, then it is your fault. Why did you create a profile, share your photos, and send likes to pictures people share? This mindset is blind to the real actor behind the scenes. This blames the victim for being naive and not studying psychology in their school.

Then these social media gurus provide small cherry-picked hacks laced in positivity and quotes to suggest that everything can be done with positive effort and belief over enough time.

This term was coined by **Lauren Bertant** in her book of the same name.

Cruel optimism is when something you desire is actually an obstacle to your own flourishing. We are accustomed to longing for things that are bad for us.

It is generally better to see the world as a nasty and unfair place, as described by Robert Greene, where you are responsible for yourself, and this will take a lot of hard work and grinding.

This forgets that every individual has a right to disconnect, which cannot be violated by any boss, corporation, or state.

After this layer, there is a third layer of **individualism and narcissism.** Current humans are more entitled and less patient than their ancestors. From childhood, they are trained to do things easily with the dial of a phone or the press of a button.

They cannot wait to play the slow game that their parents value. They want to be a billionaire or drive a Porsche. They want to become unicorns in their startups or become a bitcoin billionaires.

This has led to expectations that do not match with the lifestyle and work that require deep and slow work. Busyness is not productivity, and shallow work rarely yields exceptional results.

On the top of all, there is the concept of perpetual growth in capitalism, which is not good for the earth in the long-term. It should be replaced with steady-state sustainable growth. We cannot grow quarterly reports infinitely without incinerating our earth.

Due to this fast mindset of new humans, attention is slowly falling apart.

To redeem our attention first we must see how these factors attack and breakdown our attention.

# PART 3

# CHAPTER 12

# WHAT AFFECTS
# THE ATTENTION?

**"Too many distractions lead to a heavy mind."**
**– Naval Ravikant**

Attention can be quantified by various criteria.

Time spent in deep focus, time spent before distraction, time to catch that we have wandered, and time of intentional focus. After a distraction, we take an average of 23 minutes to return to the same level of concentration.

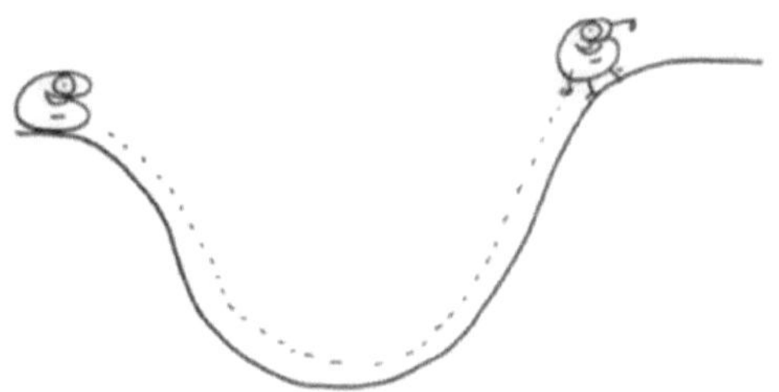

**Return to same focus after distraction**

This is too much to pay for short breaks. More information reduces focus, and fast information reduces retention.

Our attention span has reduced in recent times. It is below 40 seconds currently. It is a pity that we cannot stop ourselves from shifting our attention every 40 seconds, even if we are watching our productivity go down.

When we switch from one task to another, the transition is not smooth. There is some sticky part of the last task that stays in focus. This is called **attention residue.**

It hampers the performance in the new task. The more frequent the transition, the more residues there are to deal with. This is the switching cost that one has to bear. This term was coined by **Sophie Leroy.**

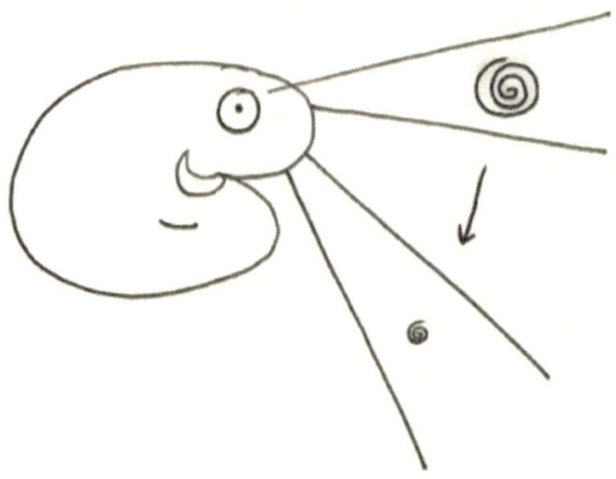

**Attention residue**

These residues frequently have open loops. They are painful and come into awareness until they are closed by a solution or a possible solution. They are like metal teeth stuck in your brain. They can turn into anxiety and rumination.

Also, when we switch between tasks, there are more errors in the work.

Also, as free space to wander and reflect is not available, hence creativity too suffers if we are changing focus frequently.

And very important for young humans who are forced to go to schools by their parents, there is less retention of information if their attention span is short.

Hence, short attention is not ideal for being productive and innovative.

Reduced attention leads to reduced reflection, which is required to analyse the circumstances and to join with each other to start a revolution to stop the wrong authority. But with no free attention left, it is almost impossible to offer resistance to even greater demands by the capitalism and state.

Let's see the place where attention works. It is our working memory. It is the part of our mental capacity that we can divert to a place of our wish. This is limited. There is a finite depth of focus that we can achieve and a finite number of stimuli that we can process at a time.

It is like the RAM (Random Access Memory) of a computer, where we play our attention game.

It can be in two modes.

Focus mode or mind-wandering mode. Both are necessary to survive in this world.

Focus can be **monastic,** in which we focus on a well-defined, clear, and discrete goal.

It can be a **bimodal** focus in which we give both deep and shallow attention. Focus can be strung into our lives depending on our work and life. One can work in deep focus on the book he is writing in his spare time while can work with shallow attention in simple repetitive tasks in the office.

If our focus is only external, then we are in autopilot mode. If it is only internal, then we are daydreaming.

This **working memory** space depends on a lot of factors.

First is our energy level. High energy leads to easier focusing.

Then another is the rhythm of our attention. Like all things in living beings, it also varies throughout the day depending on your personality.

If you are most active in the early morning, then you are a **morning lark.** And if you fire on all cylinders at 11 pm, then you are a **night owl.**

Your attention is affected by your type. As energy changes with the time of the day, so does your attention.

Most people are a mix of these two traits.

In scientific studies, attention is good between 7 to 10 am. It improves further until 2 pm. Then, it is low between 2 to 4 pm after the huge lunch we are used to taking. It gets a little better before dwindling again at 10 pm to its lowest point during sleep. At that point, we are almost dead with low batteries. So we have to match our high-value tasks to our attention level.

There is a small structure in our brainstem that secretes a night hormone called melatonin, which causes these circadian rhythms. This is affected by light, food, anxiety, and sleep deficit.

Sleep helps to grow our attention span.

Emotions regulate focus, which in turn regulates emotions. Vivid emotions create flashbulb memories as they enter in high definition into our brain storage.

Emotions can be transmitted from one human to another. This is called **emotional contagion.**

In the company of an angry or anxious friend, you may become similar. Doctors and nurses who care for patients become immune to this contagion by practice. They practice detached care, and that's why you do not find a doctor crying when he cuts through a patient during an operation. And if you find one, then you will be very anxious on his operating table.

We remember positive emotions more when we are older. This is called the **Pollyanna principle,** and it helps us stay happy even if we have been battered in life by life itself.

This positivity bias is divided into three parts – positive illusions, self-deception, and optimism.

This was derived from a novel with the same name by **Eleanor Porter,** which shows an orphan girl who tries to find happy moments in every situation.

We need both positive and negative emotions. We need negative emotions to survive and positive emotions to thrive.

When the ratio of positive to negative emotions is above 2.9, this is called the **Losada effect.** This was discovered by Marcia Losada. If positive emotions are around three times the negative emotions, it helps a person to thrive and be successful. This was refuted by some scientists, but still, we want more positive events in our psychological life.

Taking breaks between tasks and between work and life helps to replenish it.

Going into nature helps to revive weak attention. It is called **attention restoration therapy.**

**Attention restoration therapy**

Attention also depends on **willpower.** If we have an open mindset and think that we have enough willpower to focus in spite of our lazy mind, we generally focus better. Focus also affects willpower and helps in building it up.

Famous and a little bit cruel **Marshmallow test** was done by Walter Mischel. He observed kids and asked them to avoid eating marshmallows placed in front of them.

It was a study about focus and restraint. Kids had to disengage from their focus on marshmallows and resist distraction, focusing on new things like the wall of the room.

Later in life, kids with stronger control over their focus had a better life. Hence, better control of attention is a lifelong advantage.

There are four stages of distraction.

First, you are in focus.

Then you wander.

As brain areas are the same as those of focus, you generally miss this.

Then you notice that you have wandered.

Then, you bring back your focus.

Attention is peculiar in the sense that it does what we forbid it to do. If you tell your brain to avoid thinking about a pink elephant, then it cannot stop doing it. It will bring it up again and again.

When you sit down to calculate the losses you suffer due to lost attention, then you know that you could have been a billionaire if you had not given away your attention to cat videos. You need to know about two authors to see your attention from a different perspective.

# CHAPTER 13

# TWO GREAT THINKERS

## Henry Thoreau

Whatever you do has a cost. Your life. God has given you a certain unknown amount of time and attention. Whatever you focus attention on, one thing, there is an exchange. You give your attention and hence that time to that particular thing. In other words, you exchange your life for a particular piece of information.

This might put a few dollars in your pocket if you are doing this on your office computer. But it will be given away for free in exchange for getting some information floated by big digital giants. It could be a reel of a beautiful fit girl, a burning provocation by a political leader, or a new trend of dance in college guys, but this takes away some of your most precious assets.

We can call it life energy or life force.

"Most of the luxuries and many of the so-called comforts of life are not only not indispensable but also positive hindrances to the elevation of mankind."

These were the words of the famous naturalist Thoreau.

So, it is wise to know that any benefit is not a benefit. If you are able to see vacation photos of your cousins, then it is not a must to sign on Facebook. You can visit them and see their album. If you want to watch funny things to laugh at, so why not talk with your friend about all the foolish things you did in your college days? These laughs will be louder and deeper.

The second trap is small conveniences. Do not exchange your life for a little benefit that a service app or webpage provides. You do not need ten web pages to find a quote to send to your mother-in-law. Do not be part of endless groups online in which you will not notice how many of these have died during the last ten months. Stay selective.

Choose only life-changing stuff. Watch a documentary about space, the human brain, or rationality. Watch an animated movie with a cute hero. Read a Wikipedia page about a great scientist or, even better, a good biography.

Put a value on your time and give it to valuable things only.

Live an intentional life. Keep small packets of your time wrapped and give them to the traders who have the most precious things. The real things.

Let's return to Henry Thoreau. He contracted tuberculosis and became very ill. He knew the end was near; hence, he devoted his life force to things that mattered to him. He revised his works on natural history and continued his work in the forest.

He accepted his end peacefully at the age of 44. He had no restlessness for things that could have been as he had lived intentionally. His focus was always on the right things, so life seemed very peaceful and long.

## Joseph Dominguez

Once upon a time, a budding actress met a man on her road trip across America and Mexico. She found that this man was different. He was a stock analyst and had earned some money during his short career. However, he retired at 31 years of age and decided never to work for money again.

She became dumbfounded. She also started to apply his theories to her life. They lived a frugal life and managed to fulfil their monthly expenses with the income from their investments in safe treasury bonds of the government.

They showed that there is one thing called life energy, and whenever you do any work, you exchange it with your life energy. You need to count every extra second that you have to devote to preparation for your job into the total hours spent on work per week. This will give you the real hourly wage rate of your work.

They shared their ideas in the book *Your Money or Your Life*, which became a bestseller after Oprah Winfrey featured it on her show.

They showed that our time has value. Similarly, our attention is not free. It is a tool to put our time to best use. And if we waste it on fruitless pursuits, we are giving away our most precious possession. We are giving away our life force.

Who will give away such a precious possession just to watch some funny or clickbait reel which blasts a small dopamine bomb in our brain?

Joe died in 1997 due to cancer, and he showed many people that it is possible to get off the treadmill and still lead a fulfilling life.

These two humans teach us the value of focusing our life energy on true things.

Attention needs to be non fragmented to act in a reliable way when we need it. Next fable tells us exactly that.

# CHAPTER 14
# FABLE 2

**"The Hedgehog and the Fox"**

The essay

Once there was an innovative Greek poet in 680 BC who wrote poems laced with his emotions and experiences. He said this one line in one of his creations, which he wrote on papyrus, whose fragments archaeologists found. He said, "A fox knows many things, but a hedgehog knows only one big thing." Greek poet who wrote this was Archilochus.

A fable can be constructed like this.

One fox and hedgehog were friends. They were discussing life skills.

"What will you do if a lion gets you?" asked the fox. The hedgehog said, "I know only one thing. I will curl into a ball and save myself."

Fox laughed and said, "I can do many things. I can run or duck in the grass, enter the river, or enter a cave."

One day, when the lion came, the hedgehog turned into a ball. The fox was confused about what her best response would be. So, the fox became the dinner of the lion.

Focusing on our strengths saves us in difficult times.

This poetic line was refined by a Russian author in his famous essay published in 1953. He divides thinkers into two groups.

Foxes see the world and reality through the mixture of multiple ideas, unlike hedgehogs, which see and define reality through the lens of a single big idea.

Aristotle and Goethe were foxes, according to **Isaiah Berlin,** and Plato, Lucretius, and Blaise Pascal were hedgehogs.

This also applies to us. People who do multitasking are foxes, and people doing deep focused work are hedgehogs.

It is always better to be a hedgehog when you are doing work that will change your life or the lives of others.

Other times, you can be a fox juggling with many tasks and ideas at a time. No one is a pure fox or hedgehog, but a mixture of both.

The fable was described in a different way, too.

A Fox, swimming across a river, was barely able to reach the bank, where he lay bruised and exhausted from his struggle with the swift current.

Soon, a swarm of blood-sucking flies settled on him, but she lay quietly, still too weak to run away from them.

A Hedgehog happened to be passing by.

"Let me drive the flies away," he said kindly.

"No, no!" exclaimed the Fox.

"Do not disturb them! They have taken all they can hold. If you drive them away, another greedy swarm will come and take the little blood I have left."

It is better to bear a lesser evil than to risk a greater one in removing it. Hence, the central message of this fable is that we should do no further harm. When things go bad, it is time to maintain the current situation and then maybe try to improve it.

**The hedgehog and the fox**

We have already damaged our attention span by repeated overstimulation, so it is wise to stop adding new distractions and at least maintain the current attention span.

Let's try to learn how to do it by watching things around us.

# CHAPTER 15
# ART OF NOTICING

**"Focus is the art of knowing what to ignore."**
**– James Clear**

There are many things around us. When these become familiar, they become almost invisible. And you remember them when you bump into them. In the case of humans, this same thing can happen and it shake us out of stupor when that person becomes upset with us.

To train our attention, we can start to take notice of common and mundane things around us.

There is a wonderful book called *The Art of Noticing* by **Rob Walker.** The author has written short chapters about exercises to start noticing the things we miss.

## Develop the art of noticing

People who have first-class noticing ability are at the top in their field. They find the voids to fill and pains to be tackled, and these lead to successful businesses.

Alexander Horowitz described a word called **search image.**

When a songbird needs food, it searches for a particular beetle, even if other beetles are around. This is its mental search image. Practice searching for a peculiar thing in your house on your free day. A good search image leads to good destinations.

A piece of art is a form of self-expression, and it reveals the depth of mind of both the creator and the watcher. It needs slow and sustained deep noticing.

Be a child and scribble things on paper. Think in the form of images.

Hear sounds, smell things, and watch out of windows.

When on a walk, do all these things together. Feel the minute differences in things. Take pictures of things that people do not think are photo-worthy. Make videos of ruins and abandoned places.

Engage with things instead of skimming.

Eat lunch in a new restaurant. Eat lunch alone and watch other people.

Travel without Google Maps. Ask for the directions.

Read the plaque below the statues.

Travel without overspending. Celebrate the mundane. Visit less famous and less crowded places.

Watch CCTV, birds, pets, kids in laps, shops, windows, gardens, and the horizon.

If you learn to feel joy in routine exploration, then no place is boring for you.

Instead of becoming a tourist who is bound by schedule, become a flâneur who travels and drifts to new places without any pre-designed plan.

## Cues

Cues are bits of specific information that are more likely to elicit a response than nonspecific stimuli. They change thoughts and actions.

These can be small or big.

These can be external or internal.

Conscious or unconscious.

Productive or bad.

Direct or indirect.

A good cue is what forces us to do what we want to do and what we need to do.

Cue creates an impulse that enters awareness, which leads to a choice followed by action.

Cues become stronger when we are low on energy or distracted. So, our attention helps us in getting more good cues and in neglecting more bad cues.

When the cue starts to act, try to divide your actions like this.

If you can change it and it is productive, then accept it.

If you can change and it is bad, then eliminate it.

If you cannot change it and it is productive, then persevere or increase your skills to act on it.

If it is bad and you cannot change it, then accept it and wait for the right time.

**Nudges** are special cues modified or created by the more influential player in an interaction, where choices are grouped for benefit without changing financial incentives and without restricting the number of choices.

Keeping healthy food on the kitchen table and keeping a good default option are examples of nudges.

Notice how frequently life is rushing past you, and you should slow down and notice the good things in your life.

Noticing also saves lives. It warns about dangers around you. You will never hit a pole while walking. Farmers in Botswana discovered a curious thing. When they painted big eyes on the rear part of cattle, these were less likely to be attacked by wild predators. Noticing eyes can deter hungry lions, too. So start noticing things.

Now we know a lot about the science of focus and various diseases that haunt it, we need to learn how to get our foot back.

# PART 4

# CHAPTER 16

# FOCUS DURING YOUR FREE TIME

## Solution 1 – Digital detox

So we know that our focus is off. What can we do?

First principle is to reset your dopamine level. Dopamine is a brain cell messenger which is involved in pleasure, reward seeking, and motivation.

It was discovered by **George Berger** in 1910 in his lab. It was also realised by humans that it exists in our brain in 1957 by Montagu. **Carlsson** got the Nobel Prize in 2000 for discovering its importance for human behaviour.

So we can practice digital detox. It is the process of getting away from all the things that release excessive dopamine in our brain.

Detox is required for those who are addicted to digital devices.

Addiction has three components.

First, there is a loss of control over the normal and healthy use of a particular technology.

Then, there is a craving to use it, which happens even without conscious attention.

Finally, a person keeps using it even after seeing the harmful effects of it.

The away time resets these things a little bit.

Get your Wi-Fi on OFF mode and use it only for the most urgent work.

Reduce screen time to the minimum possible.

Reduce intake of alcohol and caffeine.

Reduce watching television/web series or violent news.

Walk into nature.

Talk to people who do not get on your nerves face-to-face.

Play with a pet or a little kid.

Sit with an old man who is still not addicted to smartphones.

Volunteer and do small acts of kindness.

But these techniques are short-lasting. Most of the practitioners return to their old selves very fast. They are like a festival day when your mood is through the roof and then returns to the basement the next day.

It is quite clear that digital detox is not enough in itself. Until we change our lifestyle and mindset to become the person we were born to be, these fasts are not going to help.

What these can do is to give you space. Some time to think about your life.

Why did you come out into this world from the bag of amniotic fluid? This can reconnect you to your true self. You might see glimpses of real life.

Use it intermittently when things are extreme and you are on the verge of burnout.

Or, still better, use it as a part of a better technique called digital decluttering.

# CHAPTER 17

# SOLUTION 2 – DIGITAL DE-CLUTTER

This term was explained by Cal Newport in his book *Digital Minimalism*. Here, you do not close the doors on the face of dopamine. You slowly push it out and let it wander. Then, you allow it to return to its milder and more productive form.

The first part is a digital detox in which all stimulants and technologies, except those that are absolutely necessary, are eliminated.

Then you find worthy replacements to use your free time. It should be a craft or active hobby that fulfils your free time in a healthy way.

Go into your backyard to revive that dying garden. Play carom board with your kids. Repair the damaged bookrack with tools from your garage. Cook something or sort your things. Clean that cupboard which has nesting insects.

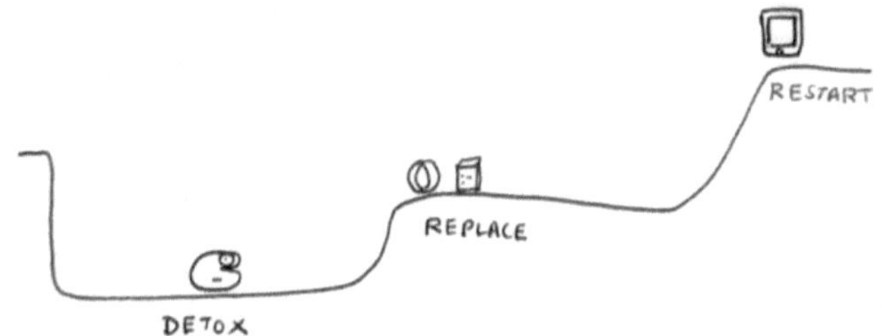


**Digital declutter**

Filling your free time with empty pursuits like watching screens leads to exhaustion and a bad aftertaste. Go out and use your hands to repair or craft something. Play outdoor games in the evening. Go into nature. Walking for some time in nature heals your attention and focus. This is called **attention restoration therapy.**

See those fascinating natural things around you. Stop to watch that beautiful tree by the side of the road that turns yellow and brown and then green every year.

Watch that little kid sitting on the lap of her mother, who finds everything beautiful.

Find your diary and scribble a few things to think clearly.

After you choose a few worthy activities, try to make them a part of your life. Make them a priority and label them as essential for your soul.

After a few weeks, pick up and scrutinise every technology that you use. Ask questions of yourself.

Should I be using it?

Is this really useful?

Amount of my life force exchanged with it?

How to avoid using it?

If not possible, how can I use it for the minimum time?

When these questions are asked, you see the real value of a particular technology.

After that, use it mindfully.

Like a monk who picks up the right thoughts and discards the wrong ones.

Use pacts to do focused work. A pact is a promise made before distractions appear. It can be a financial pact in which you pay money to charity if you fail to do deep work. It can be related to your identity, or it can be a social pact when you declare to your colleagues that this is the time when you are not available.

# CHAPTER 18

# INNER CITADEL – SOLITUDE (NOT LONELINESS)

**"Whosoever is delighted in solitude is either a wild beast or a God." – Aristotle**

This is a very moving scene for everyone. A young man in a black coat stands with his back to us. He has a stick in his hand, and his left foot is raised to land on a rock. He watches a deep layer of fog that is holding in its lap the mountains, trails, and nature.

This painting was made by the famous German artist Caspar Friedrich. He stands with confidence and without a hint of fear.

This famous picture denotes a path ahead and human reflection to see clearly through the fog. It signifies human resolve to move ahead against the most sublime forces.

When alone, be the man standing in this famous picture called Wanderer above the Sea of Fog.

**Wanderer above the sea of fog**

Solitude makes you see the challenges you are going to face and the clouds of uncertainty.

If you want solitude, you do not need to go to Point Nemo, which is the farthest place in the sea, or to go to the International Space Station.

You can practice it even in a bustling city.

Solitude is not loneliness, and it helps one to grow by providing time for self-reflection.

Loneliness is negative and isolating; it involves a longing for contact and can be harmful.

Solitude is voluntary, fulfilling, and good for health.

Loneliness can be seen on three levels.

Intimate loneliness is related to your inner circle.

Relational loneliness involves people who have a positive relationship with you and is generally limited to 50 people in your contacts.

Collective loneliness involves your whole network and is diffuse.

In Japan, there is a social phenomenon in which a person falls out of the current of society into the fringes of existence. They find it hard to mix with other humans, and it is difficult to make them a part of the whole. This is called **Hikikomori.** It harms the person.

If not done correctly, it can harm the person, as happened with Donald Crow Hurst, who left the shore for a solo sailing adventure across the world in 1968. His diary, which was recovered later, recorded his slow descent into madness.

But solitude can heal the soul if it is practiced in the right way.

According to psychologist Kenneth Rubin, solitude is productive if it is voluntary.

If the person is in control of his emotions, then solitude can help him calm down.

If he can rejoin society at will.

And if he can maintain his important relationships while being away, then there is no permanent harm.

Great minds have always blossomed in solitude. Aldous Huxley said that the more powerful and original the brain, the more it will incline towards solitude.

Lao Tzu, Moses, Nietzsche, Emerson, and Marcus Aurelius all valued alone time.

There are recorded events of people spending a very long time in solitude.

It is time free from stimuli from outside and helps to nurture focus. It is not isolation. When practising it, surrender and catch the ideas.

## Few benefits of solitude

Removes all mind-shaping influences and people's expectations.

Resets your emotions.

Gives time to reflect.

Refreshes your mind

### What to do to start it?

Decide the place.

It should be calm and distraction-free.

Schedule time

Start small and increase it gradually.

If you have little available time to do it, then practice little solitudes.

You can practice micro-solitudes when you sip your tea, go to the canteen, walk towards your car, wait for others to arrive, or drive alone.

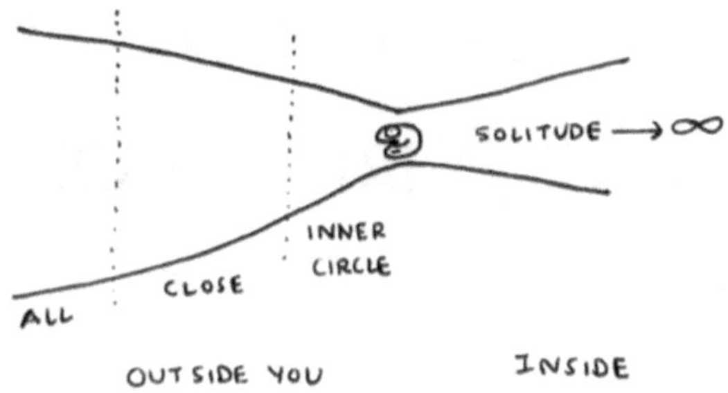


**Types of relationships and solitude**

# CHAPTER 19
# FOCUS DURING WORK

## Deep work

Focus is necessary for productivity. Productivity is an act that improves the lives of humans on earth. It is a famous word in board meetings and quarterly reports.

Busyness is not productivity. Shallow work is low-quality work done in a distracted state at superficial levels of consciousness and attention. It is not productive. Even if it is, the work is of low-quality. It can be copied by other humans and even machine intelligence.

Productivity should be aligned with sustainability to keep our planet intact after 1000 years.

Currently, humans are working on the principles of **perpetual productivity.** That means every year we will produce more than the last year, infinitely. But this is a trap. Nothing can grow infinitely in finite time. So this trend will ultimately exhaust our resources and will make Elon Musk the most essential entrepreneur. We will have to find new planets or even new galaxies.

Another mode is **sustainable productivity.** In this approach, which is followed nowhere, we produce essential things in such a way that it gives our earth time to heal and regrow.

So, let's return to deep work. Deep work requires focus at a deeper level. It is sustained focus with high-quality work and very few interruptions.

It is the work that creates masterpieces that open the mouths of the watchers.

Quality of work depends on the time given to it and the depth of the focus. This is especially true for original works that have minimal copying from other sources.

Interruptions delay the deep focus or may even obviate it.

Focus decides your reality. When we focus on positive things, life becomes more comforting. When we get older, our filters get clogged, and we neglect minor things and filter out negative stimuli. That's why older people tend to lead happier lives than young people in the same circumstances.

Deep work provides the raw material for your beliefs and mental models. These are then developed well and clearly.

Deep work can be of different types depending on how much time we devote to it.

It can **be a monastic focus** when one focuses on a discrete and clear goal with all his energy.

It can be **bimodal** when one spends a few hours in a day in a state of deep focus and the rest of the time in shallow focus.

It can be an **integrated focus** when we are flexible to incorporate it into our schedule whenever possible during the day.

Creativity requires mind-wandering, but when one sits down to capture ideas on paper, then one has to resort to deep work. You cannot grasp the full force of an idea without deep work.

When we get an idea, the execution decides its fate. We need to focus on the idea. We should find what we know very well and what is not clear. Then we need to keep track of its development and should take full responsibility to nurture it.

One interesting concept related to deep work is the **Eudaimonia machine.**

It is a theoretical conception of a perfect building to facilitate deep work. It has five connected rooms that help the person enter a deep work state.

The first room is the **gallery** to display the already finished works.

Then, there is the **coffee room** where people can meet and interact.

When we walk into it further, there is a **library** with internet where a person can do his research.

Next, there is an **office room** with a whiteboard where ideas can be crafted in small notes and iterations.

Then, we enter the last room, where deep work is done. This room is soundproof and has minimal distractions.

So, what are the options for doing deep work? Shut off your office. Keep a 'do not disturb' sign on the door when you are doing deep work. Switch off the phone.

Throw a stone towards that cat growling in the neighbourhood. Give the silicone nipple to the hungry baby. Do whatever you can do. You can use headphones with mild music or white noise.

# CHAPTER 20
# TIME MANAGEMENT

**"Time management helps in managing focus.
Stop managing time; start managing focus."**

When we are short on time, we are either hurried to do tasks at a faster pace, or we have to juggle our attention with multiple tasks. Both of these lead to bad focus and low productivity. By managing our time, we can work at a natural pace, focus on one task at a time, and allocate enough time for undistracted, deep focus on our important work.

So, without managing our time well, it is hard to improve our attention and focus.

Time is a finite thing, so we need to preserve it.

Time can be seen in two ways, like everything. One is a qualitative way. It is called **Kairos** in Greek. It is the right time. Its length matters less. A millisecond extra to a forward footballer can win millions for the team if he scores a goal. A minute of a tongue slip on national television can cost your party elections.

The right offer at the right time can close a deal for a salesman. So, this time is the right time to focus on a particular thing. You should be a good judge of the right time.

The second type of time is normal time, called **chronos.** We can quantify it with clocks, and its impact is linear. The time that we waste on reels and endless web series is chronos time. If we manage time, we partially manage our attention, as a shortage of time will not hurry our attention.

What can be done to manage it?

## Time to manage time

We should plan our time at the end of the day and at its start. Once you are trapped in a flood of tasks, planning is not possible.

## The night before the next day.

This is the time when you return to your adobe after being battered by life. You walk back into people who want good things for you and do not mind if you look like a wild hog or behave like one. Before going to bed, plan tasks for the next day.

Take the small diary in the corner drawer and write down the main tasks you need to do the next day.

Write the most vital task first and do it as the first task in the office. Then, order the remaining tasks as number 2 and 3 priority. Keep your list small. Focus on work that affects your performance and improves your skills and network.

## Office

The first step is to know where you stand before planning where you want to go. Create a chart of daily time and where you usually devote it. That is the hump of clay out of which you have to create your David.

After you are aware of your current situation, then define where you want to go. Awareness about end goals will then help to create a definite goal. If you do not know where you are going, then life will sweep you to unknown places. Places which have no road ahead and no way back home. So, write down your definite goals.

These are the things that will preserve your job or even give you a promotion.

If you are doing business, then these goals will help you to sustain your business over the long-term.

If you do not do anything, then goals will increase the chance that you will start doing something productive soon.

Then from this initial lump of data, you have created a stack of bricks to create your masterpiece. Now separate these into different heaps depending on their quality and purpose.

Then, create three lists of your tasks. Tasks that are important and have a deadline go into heap 1.

Work that is important but has no deadline goes into heap 2.

And tasks that are not important and have no deadline go into heap 3.

All the important works with big consequences go into heap one. These are to be done. Even when you get 1 second in a day, then try to do this one work. These works are 10% of the things you do but lead to 90% results.

Always do an audit of your work based on long-term consequences. Work with huge long-term consequences are the first to be engaged with. And if work has both short-term and long-term vital consequences, then it is even more important.

When you know your most important task and your goal, then **prepare** before you start.

Arrange your desk.

Close off all distractions.

Stop notifications.

Empty your bladder.

Put a 'do not disturb' sign on the gate.

Find extra pages and pens.

Keep your research notes and all necessary documents on the side.

Fill your coffee mug and start.

This work is then further chunked into smaller three parts. A three-part list of work defines the three most important skills that will do that work. Arrange these skills into one bracket. Improve these skills. Implement them. And make little daily progress towards this big work.

For example, if you want to **sell** your products, make it the main task. Then, define three tasks/skills that will be accomplished.

First is creating a clear mission statement to convey the value your product provides.

The second is creating a great pitch/advertisement to reach potential customers.

Then, there is customer care to deal with complaints and close more deals by creating positive brand value.

Other things like useless meetings and market research can be scaled down.

Sometimes works with no significant effects on your productivity and growth can be delayed until they become either important or forgotten.

Other tasks are arranged in lists 2 and 3. Works with few consequences can be delegated if possible. Other tasks are to be eliminated.

# Home

Do not carry your office to your home if possible. Home is for family and yourself. Your family is not only worthy of residual time but it deserves your prime time too.

During some free time, you can do what is called **constructive procrastination.** While doing relaxing work in your garden or on a long drive, you can let your mind go wherever it wants. This can give you some ideas about the tasks on which you are stuck in your office or business. However, it is totally involuntary, and you are not working but relaxing.

Actually, time management is energy management. We have different levels of energy and motivation throughout the day.

We need to prioritise important work when we have maximum energy and focus. And less important works can be done when our energy is low. That's why Brian Tracy advises that we should do the most important but most difficult and ugliest work first thing in the morning so that we have a good start to the day with an early big win.

Sometimes, if you have invested significant energy into a project, then you might stick to it even if it is not working. This is called the **sunk cost fallacy.**

To fight it, you can do the following things.

Do not assert ownership of this project.

Accept losses.

Embrace the fear of waste and ridicule.

Reset your budget yearly instead of accumulating long-term losses.

Avoid inertia.

Take the opinion of a knowledgeable mentor.

# CHAPTER 21

# SLOW WORK

**"Anything worth doing is worth doing slowly"**
**– May West**

This one is tricky. It is possible if you have some control over your schedule and some freedom to control your deadlines. You can do this if your work requires judgement skills and has to be of high-quality, like writing, creating music, preparing arguments for court, preparing a pitch for your startup, or choosing to invest as a venture capitalist.

These tasks need to be done at a slow pace. Slow down.

We started as fish but we are now trying to be rockets. We prefer action over poise. We value visible activity over underground growth. We have changed definitions of productivity, and we measure everything with speed. But it is due to our lack of attention.

Nature has been the same for billions of years. Everything gets done, but nature is not in a hurry. We do not see babies jumping out of their mothers in 5 months or a pine growing in a fortnight.

Things take time, and they take the time that is natural to them. We cannot shorten the time for real things. We can hasten artificial or superficial or man-made things, but nature takes its time. Physics and biology take time.

When we work without rest at our maximum capacity, then our creativity, accomplishments, and attention span fall. This results in burnout. Sustained, unhurried, slow time produces quality. It is called poetic work.

Few humans have realised it and embraced the slow revolution. Things should be done at a natural pace, which is a slow pace. Not slow in actual terms, but slow for our patience. There are slow foods, slow cities, slow media, slow cinema, and slow schools.

In the good old times, people were like nature. They took their time. Sometimes it took them decades to reveal their talents. Not like influencers these days who post every few hours. Nothing of real value gets done in a blink.

**Slow productivity**

Live a slow life.

First, find out what matters and what actually needs to be done.

Then, do fewer things. If possible, do only the most important things. When we work at full capacity for a long time without rest, our attention and productivity fall. The quality of our work is also low.

Do fewer things.

Divide them into small parts.

Take frequent breaks between strenuous work to reset focus. Take a break every 25 minutes or at least 15 minutes per hour, and the maximum gap between breaks should be less than 90 minutes. This aligns with the rhythm of our energy.

Limit the number of your missions.

Limit daily, weekly, or yearly targets.

Give away some of your control over tedious tasks and take your life back.

Put some tasks on autopilot.

Do them at the same time on the same day in one go.

Group all the tasks together according to the day, location, or people. Do all tasks related to one shop, meeting, or city together.

Take on new projects when you have enough free time. Say no before that.

Then, once you have chosen a good task, work at your own pace. Do not be a snail, but take enough breaks. Your effort should be unhurried, in chunks of sustained deep focus. When you are in flow, give five hours to it, and when it does not feel good, take some leisure time.

Add a buffer to your project. Assume the worst-case scenario and keep extra resources. One good way is to add 50% extra time to the expected finish date of a project.

Instead of only focusing on the end goals, focus on the progress. Daily small progress keeps everyone going.

Also we can do our work in the way our ancestors used to do.

# CHAPTER 22
# CYCLIC WORK

**"If you are tired don't quit but rest"**

Old humans were foragers. They worked for a few hours to gather food and water and rested for the rest of the time. Then we became farmers. We toiled throughout the day during the harvest season but rested during the off-season. Still, we worked in cycles of exertion and rest.

Then we became employees and started non-stop work. We see a desk full of coffee cups, eyes full of burning pains, and a mind spinning in its skull. We forgot the rhythms and cycles.

We came home and drowned our brains in more caffeine or alcohol and then started all over again the next day.

We continue without ever questioning if this is healing us or killing us slowly.

We need to live in rhythms. Take breaks. Frequently take relaxing breaks. The world or your company is not going to die if you splash your body on a beach.

Take enough time. Take play days. Work in cycles. During slow times, focus on the most important project and quietly quit from irrelevant tasks. Work for 4-6 weeks and then take a break. Make your happy rituals to celebrate success, like going to a luxury hotel or buying that costly hardcover and a costly cup of coffee.

When you slow down, your quality automatically improves. When we succeed, generally we try to stuff our mouth with more projects until our quality suffers. When you succeed, you should reduce your time and increase your rates.

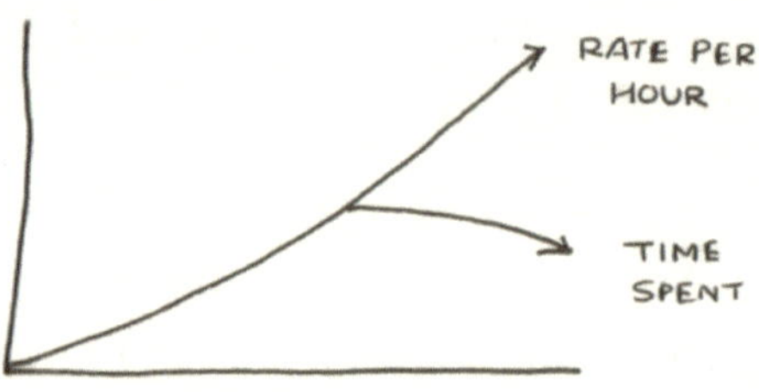


As you become famous increase
your wage per hour
and take more free time

Keep your good quality, but save yourself from this endless race to kill yourself with overwork.

Set a goal post which indicates that now you can slow down and enjoy the fruits of your hard work.

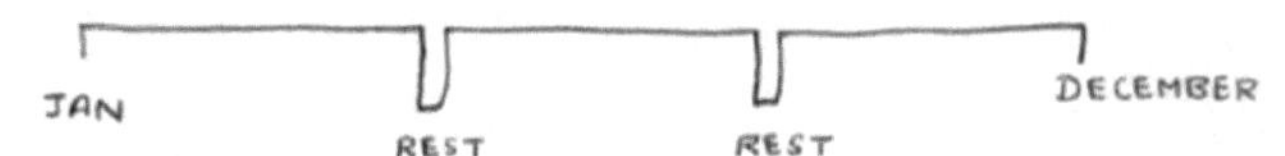


## Cyclical work

Be slow and tidy in your work. Produce the best work or service that you can create. Being skillful helps one heal.

Do work poetically. Do the work that is useful to society and that heals you. Do not always do theoretical work or practical work.

Add a buffer to all your actions. Keep extra time, energy, and resources.

There is famous fable of ant and the grasshopper. Ant worked hard in summer to store food for long and cold winters. Grasshopper did not store anything and was forced to face the painful fate.

We should work in cycles to preserve our attention and motivation for tough times and not waste away all our attentional resources well before the real test of life falls upon us. You don't want to attend your most important meeting after you have exhausted your attention stamina. Avoid burnout and make your attention muscles slowly by working in natural rhythms.

One technique for working in short cycles was described by **Francesco Cirillo.** He named this technique after the tomato-shaped timer called **Pomodoro.**

This advocates working for 20-25 minutes and then taking a break for 5-10 minutes. This restores some focus and energy. You work in cycles of 20 minutes and 10 minutes. That's why classes in schools should be shorter.

Another way is the rapid planning method developed by **Tony Robbins.**

Make a list of all your tasks. Then group tasks based on commonality. Like tasks requiring a visit to the market, tasks to be done on Monday, tasks related to investing, etc.

Do common tasks in a chunk of time after grouping them together. This is a way to focus on paper. You group tasks based on time, location, day, context, area of life, and urgency. This is especially good for works that are to be done every month and repeatedly.

Work around your energy levels. Do deep work when you are full of energy, and let your mind wander when you have low energy.

# CHAPTER 23

# MINIMALISM

**"Real happiness requires less than you think"**

He was a philosopher. He wrote encyclopedias. One day someone gifted him a scarlet gown. He was very happy. In comparison to his luxury gown, his other belongings seemed very ordinary. He purchased a new chair, desk, and other things.

This caused him a loss of great wealth. He wrote an essay on it. It was titled, Regrets of parting with my old gown.

**Denis Diderot** never imagined that his new possession would start a cycle of acquiring new possessions and would lead to debt.

This effect is called Diderot's effect. One luxury forces other luxuries to accompany it. This leads to a loss for the person.

We should avoid the Diderot effect in our lives to preserve our money and also our attention. It means reducing the number of stimuli to which you have to respond. Do less. Feel less. Stack less. Talk less. This way, you will keep your attention at peak health.

If you buy an iPhone, then the cold urge to buy an Apple Watch, MacBook, and iPad wraps you up.

Stop saying yes to everything. Stop trying to do everything. You can do anything, but you cannot do everything. Do less, but do it better.

When you start the day, set your priority. The one thing that is absolutely necessary for the day. Go easy with other things. It is the resource allocation. You have to choose where to invest your limited focus and energy. Elimination is an important part of life. Keep what is necessary.

Do one thing that is meaningful and will make the highest contribution to society.

Do the right things for the right reasons at the right time of your life.

As one intelligent author discovered, 90 percent of everything is unimportant. Hence, you have to ignore almost everything as you go about your life. Be the best editor and keep essential things only.

Avoid the traps of victim mentality and learned helplessness.

When we feel overwhelmed and helpless, then we do one of these two things.

We give up and sit on our sofa, listening to the latest sad numbers.

Or we may become overactive to compensate and try to do too many things at a time. Both of these hurt our attention.

Everything has an attention trade-off. If you focus on one, then you miss millions of other things. No one can escape this thing. One can make trade-offs deliberately and strategically but cannot delete them.

As Thomas Sowell said, "There are no solutions, only trade-offs."

The busier we are, the more free time we need to reflect on where we should head in the future. The essence of information is vital.

Write down the list of all the things that you can throw. Stop adding any non-essential things.

Know these truths –

There is a lot of noise.

You can do lots of things, but not everything.

You can do anything, but not everything.

Choose a place to focus your energy and time.

Accept the trade-off of every decision.

A summary, a story, or a single word can convey the message.

Your life mission should be concrete and inspirational.

Try to gather the essence of the information. Write down to extract the gist.

Choose one important thing that is concrete, clear, and inspires you.

Say no frequently and say it correctly. Say no firmly and gracefully. Seek respect in place of popularity.

When you focus on the most important thing in life, do not fall into the trap of reaching the goal before enjoying your life. Enjoy the journey to make life worth living, even if it is not very long.

**Let's see how to say "No" in the right way.**

Take pause. Always take your time. Don't reply in a hurry.

Say, let me get back to you.

Never reply on the spot. Say, "Let me check my calendar."

Say I am willing for something other than what you offer.

Say that one common friend may be willing instead of you.

Say no firmly and gracefully.

Try to win self-respect in place of popularity.

A clear "No" is better than a vague "Yes."

Always keep in mind that you should say "Yes" slowly and "NO" very fast.

If it is still not possible to avoid, dedicate a minimum amount of time to the meeting or task.

Do not go for perfection. Good enough does it most of the time. Produce the minimum viable product, ship it, and then improve with feedback.

Work smarter instead of working harder. Go from the trivial many to the vital few things.

# CHAPTER 24

# ALDOUS HUXLEY'S PARROTS

He had a sharp mind. He was diagnosed with oral cancer but still put up a fight for two years.

He was like a slowly sinking ship with all lights shining brightly, as his friend remarked when he met him in the hospital. He was famous, but his death was noticed less due to the assassination of John F. Kennedy six hours before his death and the death of another great author, C. S. Lewis, on the same day.

Aldous Huxley was a legendary author. In his last work, he imagined a utopia on an island in the middle of the sea. An English sailor got there after his ship got wrecked.

Here, the author correctly finds that attention will be the most important thing in the future. It will decide who wins and who gets beaten. On this island, birds fly in the sky and remind everyone throughout the day to pay attention. "Pay attention. Here and now," they repeat endlessly.

This brings everyone to the present for some definite amount of time.

We need such birds in our sky.

One similar thing is the **Mindfulness bell.**

Famous Vietnamese monk who lived in Plum village of France describes it beautifully. Zen Master **Thich Nhat Hanh was** a global spiritual leader, poet, and peace activist, revered around the world for his pioneering teachings on mindfulness and peace.

It is a bell that rings at frequent intervals. It lasts for many seconds and feels soothing to the ears. This is a sign to return to self and to return to the present.

It is a simple way to train your mind to be present. It is a metallic bell that, when chimed, creates a soothing, long sound. Keep it around you.

Even apps are available that produce the sounds of a mindfulness bell at regular intervals. Whenever it rings, stop whatever you are doing if the task can be stopped. Return to the present. Breathe and observe your surroundings. It releases tension and trains your mind to face boredom with a little ease.

Another way to see this bell is to be a bell yourself. Whenever you see your friend or family suffering, then be a mindfulness bell.

Get in touch and remind them again and again that time is tough, but life is beautiful, and it will blossom again. You need to say things that will heal the person, and you have to repeat this a few times for a few days.

# CHAPTER 25

# FOCUSING WHILE INSIDE YOUR SKULL

**"Focus and simplicity. Once you reach it, you can move mountains." – Steve jobs**

**D**onald Hebb wanted to be a novelist, and he even got a degree in arts. But he was destined to be an eminent neuroscientist who studied neural networks.

In spite of the death of his two wives and difficulties in university, he gave the concept called **Hebb's law.** It states that neurons that fire together wire together. This creates habits and memories.

So, similar and repeated stimuli coming into attention can create strong memories and then strong habits.

You are not your brain. The physical brain is the receptor that receives the stimuli. The real you, who is the observer and experiencing part, is the real one. You have veto power to change your response to incoming stimuli.

There is a non-healthy input in your attention, like thought, urge, impulse, desire, or sensation.

It creates a feeling of uneasiness. It can be in the form of uncomfortable emotion or just a sensation of discomfort.

You cannot stop these inputs from rising, but you can control your response to them.

You can go to the usual unhealthy response to discomfort, like distracting yourself with food, screens, or chemicals. You can also choose a healthy response instead.

Emotions are not bad, but the urges that you form due to your response to them cause all the damage.

For example, the loss of close ones leading to grief and sadness is a healthy response. One should honour it. But self-sabotaging, cursing yourself, and self-hatred is not a healthy way to deal with loss.

Similarly, focusing on anxiety is not always bad as it is a signal to guide you towards priorities, but rumination and magnified anxiety are destructive. Accept it and then detach from its identity.

Or you can try healthy alternatives like mindfulness and reflection.

Attention plays a big role in this self-control. You cannot stop these inputs, but you can work around them. Focus on a specific part of the event helps you in creating a healthy response. Wait out these or accept and face.

**Mindfulness** is non-goal-directed, non-judgmental acceptance and observation of the present.

Watch and let the input be as it happens. Instead, watch your response to it. If it is unhealthy, then try to modulate it.

Instead of believing your false self-called ego, try to be ego-dystonic. Do not believe it blindly and do not fuse with it.

One good way is to wait for a few minutes before acting on unhealthy urges.

So our inward focus is a complex interaction of thoughts and emotions. You need to learn healthy ways to focus on these thoughts and urges which arise frequently.

**Ways to focus on your inner world.**

Choose empowering thoughts that do not make you a victim.

Thoughts should be free from complaints.

Thoughts should be positive.

Thoughts should be big.

Thoughts should be free from mental distortions.

**Ways to increase the power of your inner focus**

Practice meditation daily. It can be walking meditation, sitting meditation, yoga, group meditation, or morning meditation.

Observe and write your prominent thoughts and moods in a journal at the end of the day. Improve their quality with time.

Pause before acting on an urge.

Know that you are the watcher who can modify many things in your inner space.

Always keep your thoughts that will help you grow and be happy in the long-term.

Go on a Vipassana retreat during one of your sabbaticals.

Listen and read great books about thoughts.

Sleep like a child and rest in between.

You can also practice **emotional agility,** which was coined by psychologist Susan David.

It involves four steps and is adapted from acceptance and commitment therapy.

First, make a list of your core values in life.

Then, see patterns of your response to your thoughts and emotions. Do you reflect or pounce on these like a wild hound?

Then label them. Call them by their names.

Accept all thoughts and emotions.

Work on them according to your values.

# CHAPTER 26
# BOREDOM

**"Boredom always precedes period of great creativity"**

Boredom is a mismatch between expectations and the level of current stimulation. It is not a new phenomenon, but it has increased in recent times and has filled every second of human time when he is not sleeping.

God has made us in such a way that we have to sit doing nothing. But we have taken that to be wasted time. We fill this time with whatever is available in that instant. These negative, violent, and rapid stimuli spoil the poise of even the most serene person.

When we pick up the phone in the lift when our food order is coming or when the person next in line has forgotten his PIN number for online payments, we surrender to these reflexes.

These **gaps** in the experience leave us vulnerable to checking our phones. Then, this becomes a malady as we check our phones even when we are driving our car on a busy highway.

We lose our battle with distractions during these small gaps. These are to be watched carefully. Instead of getting sucked into your phone when you are waiting for the taxi to come or using the toilet, try to return to the present and observe the wonderful surroundings around you.

Finding short bursts of distractions trains our minds to be restless. It says that it is normal to seek novelty in every second.

Embrace boredom. Sometimes, sit without doing anything. Sit in your backyard, staring at the sky. Read the long fiction book that is being eaten slowly by moths.

**Embrace boredom**

Pick up papers in your room and arrange them in place. Make your bed and adjust your room.

Go through your old papers and separate them into useless and useful ones.

Wait for the person you expect to meet without looking at the phone. See your kids playing in the park while you do nothing.

Sit for meditation or visit a temple in your area. Boredom is the antidote for hyperactivity. It is normal to be bored sometimes.

Boredom helps you to practice productive mind-wandering. Do habitual and boring work like rearranging your bookshelf. This leaves enough mental space for reflecting on your life and maybe to capture a few good insights floating inside.

The same thing can be done on a long drive on a freeway or walking on a park trail.

You need to learn to surf the urge. Whenever you get an urge to do something which is not in your best interest, follow the **10-minute rule.** Wait for 10 minutes before acting on it. This trains your resolve.

It sounds counterintuitive to the 5-second rule given by **Mel Robbins,** in which you act within 5 seconds. But that is for taking action on things which are vital and productive for you, but due to fear, you are not acting on them. It is not for every impulse that crosses your mind.

Be a mindfulness bell for others. Remind your family and friends as they drown in their screens that reality exists outside, and they need to come back home.

Be the **Whistler's Mother** when you have nothing to do. Remain calm and watch things around you with no visible pain. This picture was made by artist James Whistler, and it has been mentioned in countless movies and books, including in a movie about Mr. Bean.

**Whistler's mother**

It shows that sitting still for some time without expecting any reward or stimulation is possible. Print it and put it on your desk.

# CHAPTER 27

# LEISURE

**"We need leisure to create and dream"**

Leisure is free time when a person does not do things that he doesn't want to do. It is perceived as freedom from the compulsions of routine life. These activities are done for their own sake and are not linked to productivity, although they may increase the skills of the person.

Recreation is not the same as leisure, and it is a purposeful activity done in free time.

If you want to read the best poem on leisure, then read the poem by **William Henry Davies.**

It goes like this...

What is life full of care?

We have no time to stand and stare.

No time to stand beneath the boughs,

And stare as long as sheep and cows:

No time to see when woods we pass,

Where squirrels hide their nuts in grass:

No time to see, in broad daylight,

Streams full of stars, like skies at night:

No time to turn at Beauty's glance,

And watch her feet, how they can dance:

No time to wait until her mouth can

Enrich that smile her eyes began?

A poor life this, if full of care,

We have no time to stand and stare.

It was written in 1911 and caught the imagination of the public.

Leisure can be of different types.

It can be a hobby, which is a voluntary, fulfilling, and interesting activity. It can increase skills.

Leisure can be in the form of bricolage and DIY (do-it-yourself) activities.

It can be casual, like watching television.

It may be done for the sake of display and social status and practiced by the rich people. These are the people who increase the demand for costly goods with an increase in their prices. These are called **Giffen**

**goods** and violate the principle of demand and supply. Examples are costly wines, perfumes, and luxury cars.

High-quality leisure has certain properties.

It increases skills.

It re-energises and provides relaxation.

It connects people.

It gives space for reflection. According to **Bennett's principle,** leisure should be active, and it leads to more fulfilment and rejuvenation.

Crafting something gives a feeling of self-efficacy and autonomy. These are good for the soul.

# CHAPTER 28

# FOCUS WHEN YOU ARE NOT AWAKE

**"Sleep solves most things"**

## Shut-down rituals

Every machine needs off time. It is switched off, and slowly, its engine dies down so that it can recover its gears in the off time. We are the same. We need to develop a shut-down ritual at night so that we can sleep well and restore our attention. Develop your ritual, but do not go to bed arguing with a stranger about the latest meme.

Shut off your windows. Make the night dark. Use less bright lights. Shut off your screens. Keep the tea and coffee cans away.

Go outside and see the night which is coming down slowly. Seeing darkness is healing at the end of the day. It signals to your brain that you did well today and now sleep can crawl over you to heal you.

It is as important as going into the morning sun after you get up. It is a natural way to start and end your days that our ancestors always followed.

One important thing is to put an end to unclosed loops. Write down tasks or things bothering you and write possible solutions to them. This will make these loops wriggle less during the night.

Reading a nice book may be the best way to rest. It releases no radiation and slowly taps you to sleep.

Say, thank you to the universe for gifting you one more day.

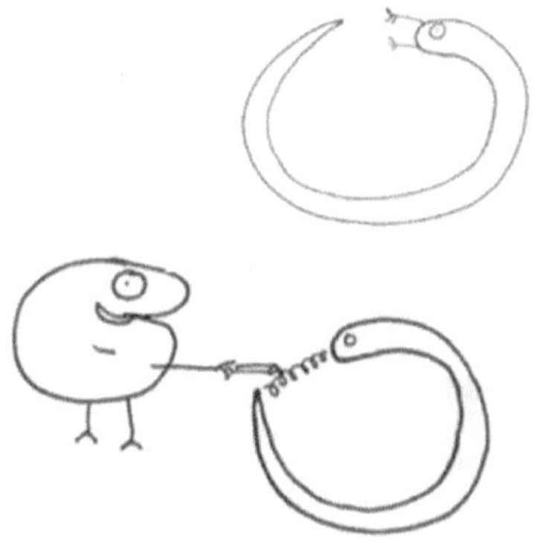

**Close the open loops**

## Sleep

Sleep is the thing that consumes a big part of our lifetime, but we are still unsure why we sleep. Life probably started in a sleeping position millions of years ago, and evolution crafted sleep to fit each species. Birds can sleep with half their brains at a time, and sea animals can go without sleep for a long time.

But mammals need to sleep. Our ancestors slept in two phases – a night sleep and an afternoon nap.

When we are awake, a molecule called adenosine builds up in our brain, which creates pressure to sleep. Then comes the melatonin hormone to declare that it is dark and it is time to sleep. We keep pushing away the adenosine pressure with coffee and tea. It harms our physiology.

Sleep has an early part in which eyes do not dart, and this part reflects on the inputs we gather during wake time. This is non-REM sleep.

And phase called REM sleep in which eyes dart in their sockets and we dream as our muscle tone goes down. This phase consolidates our memories. Getting up earlier than 7-8 hours affects our REM sleep mainly.

When deprived of sleep, our attention and focus are affected, and our creativity falls. Chances of heart disease, diabetes, dementia, and accidents increase.

**Things that we know can help us in sleeping and hence becoming the best version of ourselves.**

Set a bedtime and waking up time. Routines help in maintaining healthy sleep.

Do not take an afternoon nap after 3 p.m.

Avoid coffee, tea, alcohol, and nicotine in the second half of the day.

Exercise, but not in the later half of the day.

Take a shower in the evening.

Do not have a heavy meal at dinner.

Do not sit in bed if you are not sleepy.

Do some relaxing and easy tasks like reading and telling stories to kids.

Keep voices and screens away from the room and reduce lights.

Expose yourself to the sun in the morning and darkness in the night.

Keep a gratitude journal.

Avoid chronic use of sleeping pills.

**Follow the 10-3-2-1 rule.**

Ten hours before sleep, avoid caffeine.

Three hours before sleep, avoid heavy food.

Two hours before sleep, relax.

One hour before sleep, switch off bright lights and blue screens.

# CHAPTER 29

# BEHIND MOUNTAINS ARE MOUNTAINS

**"Focus is a matter of deciding what things you are not going to do." – John Carmack**

## Where to focus?

So we reach the end and stand still on the verge of finishing a short conversation. It was about things we give our attention to. But that is not the only thing we are concerned with. We also want traces to stay after reality has shifted its place.

Humans die. Corpses rot or burn. Then, they are carried by the winter wind and flushed with little trails of water towards the endless oceans.

Everything chases other things, and when a thing has left, there is a transient existence that another person can feel.

You can see it in the warmth of a recently vacated seat.

Feel the aftertaste of a good beverage.

Hear the rhyming of a recently ended tone.

Scent of a bakery after it has closed down for the night.

These are called **infrathin.**

These are things that stand between two states of being. These are things that we know and can explain, but we cannot define.

These are things we like, and they say, "I was here." These are the freshest memories of a good thing that has just ended.

This term was coined by scientist **Marcel Duchamp.** So, we live in a world where we miss infrathin.

If we start to notice these afterimages or sounds or feelings, then we become more sensitive to reality.

Watching the invisible sensitises the senses. We learn to focus well if we can focus on the after-effects of an event.

Marcel Duchamp was a French painter who pioneered plastic art. He had a great impact similar to Picasso and died peacefully in his home due to heart failure in 1968. His tomb had the following words written on it, "Besides, it is always the others who die."

Another thing that can help us recover our attention is **allokataplaxis.** It is a word coined by beard-wielding ecologist **Liam Heneghan.**

It is a feeling of fascination in the ordinary.

When we go to a tourist place, things are the same. Same concrete, roads, and trees, but there we feel heightened enjoyment and solace. Noodles there taste better, and tea has more aroma in it.

If we can transfer some of these feelings to our daily lives, then it will build our attention muscle.

Most of the time, our attention is fixated on things we want and things we want to avoid. But there is another realm beyond these.

This realm of being aware of the transience of events and the shortness of life. Nothing lasts. Neither the victory nor the loss. Neither kings nor states nor ideologies. Everything changes. A truth at one point in time can become a lie in another place.

So it is most sane to focus on the only thing we have: focus on the **present.**

Stand in a flowing river of time with attention to the present moment only. What will come and what has flown by are mostly beyond your control and planning.

You can control your attention and direct it to the most real thing in front of you, and that is the present moment.

Be like **Mount Fuji.** There is a very famous picture made by Japanese artist **Hokusai.** It shows the way to be.

In it, there are two things to focus on one side, there is a beautiful but imposing big wave arising from the sea. It has curves like little claws at its end. And in the background is Mount Fuji.

Wave denotes the chaos of life that surrounds everyone, and Mount Fuji shows a calm and resolute soul who knows that the wave is going to pass after some time.

Try to be like that mountain.

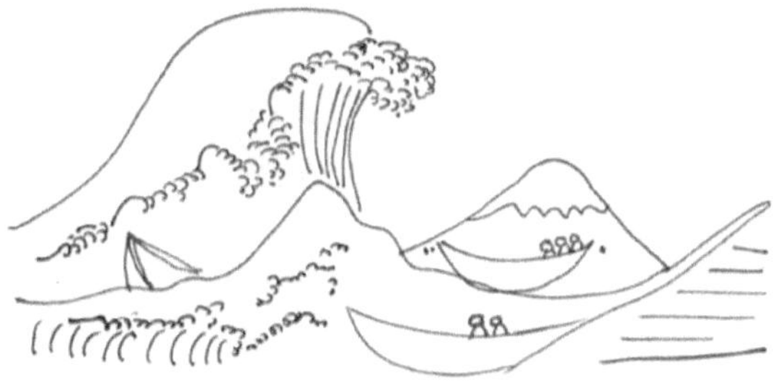

**Be the mount Fuzi**

Or, still better, try to be the **eye of a hurricane.**

Cyclones are violent spurts of our weather. They damage everything in their path. The eye is a small part in the center of a cyclone, which is very calm compared to the carnage around it. It can trick unsuspecting residents into coming out thinking the cyclone has passed and thus facing the other end of the eye.

Try to be like the eye of the storm, which stands immobile in the center of speed. Be a man who remains sane when everyone else is losing their mind. Focus all your attention to create a space of calm around you by controlling your thoughts and your responses.

**Peter Seville** was a graphic designer who crafted covers of music albums. He picked up an astronomy book from Cambridge and stumbled upon a graph by scientist **Harold Craft.** It was a graph that showed stacked recordings of radio pulses from a pulsar. A pulsar is a remnant of a star that is violently revolving, and it is a Neutron Star.

He took this graph as inspiration and put it over the cover of the album *Unknown Pleasures* by the band Joy Division. This image became iconic.

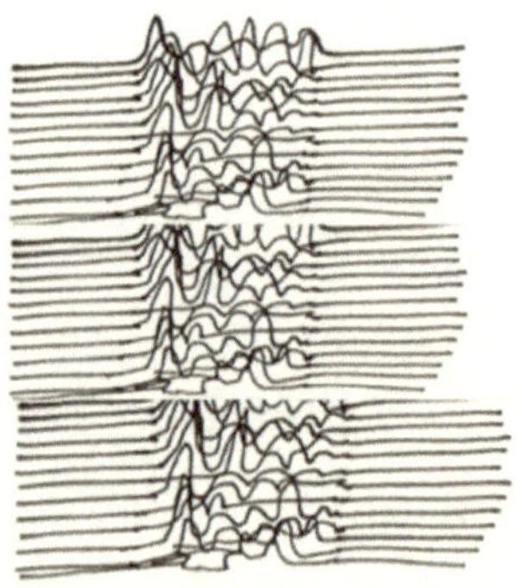

**Behind mountains are mountains**

It has a different interpretation. It appears like a row of mountains behind mountains. You cross one, then you will face another similar imposing mountain. It is a lot like human life.

Know the truth that you should not over focus on problems in front of you as you will agree that there is no permanent end to our problems. Focus on the present and know that problems are to be worked around.

Always remember this Haitian proverb that says, 'Beyond mountains are mountains.'

One problem is replaced by the next problem, or it returns or changes its form, or we become weaker compared to the problem in front.

So there is never going to be a time when problems will all end. So it is better to focus our attention on a happy path instead of happy goals. That will reduce a few of the burdens that hang over your soul.

This iconic image can also represent happiness. Waves of happiness are not linear. There are dips of sadness and grief with peaks of exhilaration. If there is a graph to represent life, then this picture will be a worthy candidate for this. Life has cycles of regular ups and downs until it stops at either end.

# CHAPTER 30
# RESPECT CAN SAVE US

**"Focus is about saying no." – Unknown**

We are social beings who need each other to survive. We get close to each other, then we are called family or friends. A little apart, we become neighbors and colleagues. Still far, we become strangers. And if we are close but not fitting with each other, then we become enemies.

We are thus in relationships. These are not perfect. These are all tentative. These are like a piece of rope held by two people at two ends. It has to be cared for continuously from both sides.

Today, our attention has shifted from the person in front of us. Only residual attention is available for our relationships.

We are like hedgehogs. We try to get close to each other when winter gets harsher and summers become unbearable. We seek the touch of real human nerves to soothe our burning nerves. We seek the proximity of a human to calm our heart. We need someone to speak these words slowly and with confidence that everything will be fine.

If we hear this from someone we trust, it heals many things in our broken souls.

But due to our divided attention, we face the hedgehog's dilemma. It was described by a great philosopher.

He was the most important philosopher until the First World War. He became even more famous after his death.

He was read by Einstein, Pauli, and Schrödinger, who are the fathers of quantum physics. He wrote this little fable to show that we cannot have a perfect relationship. If we get too close, we hurt each other like hedgehogs. We have to keep a little distance and have tentative relationships. Schopenhauer described human relationships in a short fable.

## Fable 3

The concept of the Hedgehog's dilemma originates in the following parable from the German philosopher Schopenhauer.

One cold winter's day, a number of porcupines huddled together quite closely in order to share their mutual warmth and prevent themselves from being frozen. But they soon felt the effect of their quills on one another, which made them move apart again.

**The hedgehog dilemma**

Now, when the need for warmth once more brought them together, the drawback of the quills was repeated so that they were tossed between two evils until they had discovered the proper distance from which they could best tolerate one another.

Thus, the need for society, which springs from the emptiness and monotony of men's lives, drives them together; however, their many unpleasant and repulsive qualities and insufferable drawbacks once more drive them apart.

The mean distance that they finally discover and that enables them to endure being together is politeness and good manners. By virtue thereof, it is true that the need for mutual warmth will be only imperfectly satisfied, but on the other hand, the prick of the quills will not be felt.

Yet whoever has a great deal of internal warmth of his own will prefer to keep away from society in order to avoid giving or receiving trouble or annoyance.

– Schopenhauer (1851)

So we need each other to be close enough but not very close. On the contrary, we have developed needles like hedgehogs by focusing our attention on something other than the person in front. We disrespect that person, and if both are doing it, then they disrespect their relationship.

Respect can save us. We need to be good listeners and watchers. Sit in front of another human with your full body and mind. Converse as if he is the last person on earth after the apocalypse. Do not let dopamine spurts from your phone make you disrespectful towards fellow beings.

This will bring about the reality in front of you and will help you see clearly where you have come from and where you need to go.

**Sonder** is a good word to know how to see others. Realise that everyone, including that stranger on the street, has a vivid and complex life like your life. Everyone is fighting something and trying to move towards something. Once you see that, you start to develop the wonderful skill of empathy. **Empathy** is what keeps humans glued together on this planet.

When we are deprived of human touch and attention, then we start to die. What I am going to share now may be a poignant ending, but it is necessary.

Japan is a developed country where one in every four citizens is above 60 years old. Here, there is a new business which is cementing its foothold.

The business is to restore the rooms where some person has died a lonely death. People are dead for a long time before a sudden **discovery** leads somebody to inquire about the silence or smell of decay in a particular house. Sometimes, the landlord comes after months to collect the rent.

There, he finds a rotting corpse and silently watches the belongings that we work our whole lives to accumulate.

Only living things are flies and maggots if this happens to be the summer season. Company people who are dealing with the task of disposing the body work like a professional team to pack the leftovers in plastic bags.

Imagine a person who is welcomed by enthusiastic parents and relatives is left to rot alone in the later part of their lives in the middle of a busy city. No one to remember the name that parents had given to that person, and no one to look at the pictures he had clicked with so much zeal.

It is time to focus on the right things. If we lose this battle, then generations will be wounded. Technology will win over biology and its fragile belongings.

Let's end our conversation with a hard hitting mindset.

**"If you can't change it, you gotta stand it."**
**Annie Proulx**

# PART 5
# APPENDIX

# CHAPTER 31

# HOW TO FIGHT
# YOUR PHONE

There are a few basic principles that can help you.

## Keep it away

When a phone is not required to save your life, job, or the world, then keep it out of your reach. It is the most effective strategy.

When you sleep, keep it in another room. Do not use it as an alarm. Keep a landline for emergency calls.

When going out with friends, swap phones with them, and do not tell your PIN to them.

When you go out for a stroll or evening walk, then leave it at home. The world is not going to explode if you are not available for some time.

When you cannot keep it in another room, then activate the airplane mode to keep the notifications away.

## Keep an intermediary

Use a watch to answer calls or a band. It will save you from getting drowned in the email box or reels while checking the notifications.

Use Alexa or another AI assistant to answer the calls or play music.

Keep an assistant in your office to receive your calls and then filter them out for your time.

Make your partner put a PIN on the most abused app and then, with his help, open it for a limited time.

## Use Lego mode

Rearrange the apps. Keep the bad and time-consuming apps in the slow poison folder.

Keep banking apps, email, productivity, and learning apps in different folders. This serves as a regular reminder about bad places to visit on your phone.

## Make it ugly

Make the phone unbearably ugly. Activate grayscale as it reduces the novelty and magnetism of media. Set a PIN for all bad apps so that you have to put in an effort to open them.

Use bad websites in a browser so that they are less functional.

Log out of bad websites after every session of use and log in every time you revisit.

## Make it useless

Delete the bad apps.

Reduce the number of total apps.

Delete apps after use if you do not need them daily.

## Strangle the throat

Make your phone mute.

Limit the notifications.

Only your bank apps and incoming call notifications are enough. Every other notification is superfluous and costly.

## Reverse time travel

Purchase a cheaper and simpler phone. A phone with big buttons only will do. A phone that is to be used for taking calls only.

**Put locks** – Put a PIN on all bad apps.

## Make small pieces

Use a different device for different tasks.

A phone is for making calls only.

A desktop is for watching movies and series for a limited fun time.

An alarm clock is there to wake you up. Reduce the number of new gadgets and accessories. A band, watch, or a smart speaker, if not used wisely, can waste a lot of time.

## Decide fun time

You are on earth for a limited time and so sometimes can be devoted to enjoying a good movie or video. Fix time for that and do not break the limited time to indulge in your phone.

## Mind the boring gaps

Do not pull the phone out. When you are waiting for a lift, waiting for a taxi, sitting inside a taxi, or going to the washroom, fight the temptation to pull the phone out. Consider your phone like a gun that you cannot pull out if you are dealing with or surrounded by human beings.

# CHAPTER 32

# HOW TO ESCAPE
# THE INTERNET AND EMAIL

First of all, disable email notifications.

Check your email when you are ready and have time to deal with it.

Decide on a fixed time to check. Check at fixed times and allocate a fixed amount of time to manage all new emails.

Go on binge-checking and answer at that time.

Push all unnecessary emails into the spam folder.

Create folders for priority and routine emails.

Write short emails. Use premade templates.

Use two emails: one private email for your family, friends, banks, core business, and urgent contacts. The other is a public email for everyone.

Answer with short emails.

Delegate your account if it is too heavy and can be delegated.

Clean the inbox regularly and delete waste mail.

Create default reply emails. Use the 'out of office' label.

Few tools help you pause your email.

Unsubscribe from social media emails, useless newsletters, and promotional emails.

# CHAPTER 33
# EMBRACING SELF

**"Conquering self is the biggest war" – Vipassana**

Imagine you are locked in a building with a person who is very strange. He knows every bad and immoral thing you have ever done.

He knows all the sins you have done and all the lies you have told. He has a list of all the promises you have broken and all the things you are afraid of.

He knows all your body parts that hurt and all the places that itch. He knows every thought you are about to have.

You can't hurt him or lock him out of your room. You cannot call the police to take him away or punch him in the face.

Living with oneself is a very difficult task. We need the lubrication of society to tolerate ourselves. Living face-to-face with yourself can be a frightening and unpleasant experience.

That's what you do in Vipassana. You stay alone with yourself and other similar people, living silently with themselves inside the four walls of a retreat.

Vipassana was taught by Buddha. S.N. Goenka was born in Burma and received training in Vipassana from his teacher Sayagyi for 14 years. Then he spread his teachings to other people.

This makes you observe things as they are. You compete with yourself for ten days.

It starts with **sila,** which means morality.

You cannot kill, tell lies, steal, get intoxicated, or have promiscuous relationships. These are the five precepts of sila.

You cannot read, write, talk, or make communication except during allowed times or emergencies.

For the first three days, you focus on your breath, and this is called **anapana** meditation.

Then you practice Vipassana. In it, there are various techniques to scan your body and become aware of bodily sensations without judgement.

During this, there are determined hours during which you do not move, even if your body hurts.

On day 10, you start to talk again. This is the day you practice **metta bhavana,** which means the feeling of loving-kindness.

This ends the retreat. You are not Superman or Spiderman after this. But you learn that you can live with yourself and even be happy about it.

The more you are comfortable with loneliness and yourself, the less the urge to numb your senses from the sensations of self.

# CHAPTER 34

# HOW TO READ MORE BOOKS AND LEARN

**"Think before you speak. Read before you think."**

Books are a type of focus gifted to us by someone else. Authors work hard on certain things that bother them, and they want to express them to others. They create fiction or non-fiction to tell how they see reality.

When you read a book, you are feasting on the fruits of productive focus by the author, who might be long gone. The author invests their focus to harvest great ideas.

Books show the power of giving attention. When a reader reads a book with full attention, he gets the taste of a particular perspective on a topic. Hence, books are an exchange and storage of attention.

Reading is a strong tonic for focus.

**So, how to read more books?**

First, you should have some interest in reading and awareness of the deep benefits of reading.

Go to a peaceful place in your house.

Start with whatever you like. Start small. Ten pages a day will do.

No books are better or worse than others as long as they do not teach you ways to harm society.

Read small books.

Read books that other people are reading. Books that pull you like magnets.

Read on vacation, breaks, trains, parks, and during gaps in your busy times.

Join a reading club or reading challenge like the Goodreads Reading Challenge.

Read multiple books at a time to keep the interest up.

Quit any book that clogs your mental flow.

**Now, let us see how to read a book faster.**

Do not vocalize what you are reading in your mind. (Subvocalizing)

Use a pen or a marker to keep you on track so that you do not reread the same words. (Regression)

Use the correct font while reading.

Scan the book before starting, and do not read non-essential parts like dedication and acknowledgements.

Read more as it increases the reading speed.

Carry books on vacation or a trip.

Buy an e-book reader and use it when lights are out and others are sleeping.

When working on some routine tasks, then listen to the audiobooks. It frees your hands. Slowly increase the speed of the audiobook to listen to more books in less time. This is generally possible with non-fiction books.

Share what you read.

Read with others and exchange books.

Take notes from the books you read.

Use highlighters and scribble on the sides.

Read great books again and take notes a second time.

Gift books and receive books as gifts.

Read more to train your attention.

Use your spare pennies to buy more books.

Information you gather from books should also be intentional.

Read books that give actionable and inspiring information with a long shelf life. They should add to your existing knowledge and increase the level of your skills. The content should be interdisciplinary and help you achieve your goals.

# PART 6

# CHAPTER 35

# WORKBOOK

**W**orkbook for Improving Your Focus

How do you rate your current overall focus?

List the top three things that waste your time.

1.

2.

3.

Write one way to reduce time in each of these by half.

1.

2.

3.

How can you use the time you recover in such a way?

1.

2.

3.

Do these every day and record your progress.

Notice three things around you whenever you feel the urge to pick up the phone.

Download a mindfulness app and set the bell to ring every 30 minutes. Take three mindful breaths whenever it rings.

Take a short walk in your room.

List one person who wastes your time on unproductive tasks.

Write a few ways in which you can reduce this time wastage.

1.

2.

3.

Write down three apps related to productivity that you cannot work without.

1.

2.

3.

Delete all other apps from your phone.

List things you can do to make your phone less attractive.

1.

2.

3.

4.

5.

Do these now.

What are the gaps in the day when you automatically take out your phone?

1.

2.

3.

4.

5.

How do we tackle this problem with gaps?

1.

2.

3.

Write the number of hours in a day that you focused up to the level you wanted.

Write the first thing that you do when you get up, and is this productive?

List five places where you can go without your phone.

1.

2.

3.

4.

5.

When are the times when you can switch off your phone?

1.

2.

3.

What are the tasks that you can take away from your smartphone?

1.

2.

3.

4.

5.

Label all apps that suck your time and energy and put these in the toxic folder.

1.

2.

3.

4.

5.

Delete apps that you use very infrequently and uninstall them every time after use, then reinstall them the next time you need them.

Can you do it with a feature phone, and can you let go of a smartphone?

Block time for fun browsing each day, and do not exceed that.

List five things to do to avoid using your phone when meeting other humans.

1.

2.

3.

4.

5.

List the last thing you do when going to sleep and ask if it is good for you.


List five moments when you feel the flow and are not using a smartphone.

1.

2.

3.

4.

5.

Can you use your phone to take calls only?

List five good things that you can do in the time that you get from phone use.

1.

2.

3.

4.

5.

Note the duration you give to each of these during the day.

1.

2.

3.

4.

5.

Walking

Reflection

Solitude

Reading

Deep conversation

Crafting

Exercising

Laughing

Note down the times of day when you have the most energy.

1.

2.

3.

**Recommended books**

Focus by Daniel Goleman

Stolen Focus by Johann Hari

Indistractable by Nir Eyal

Digital Minimalism by Cal Newport

Deep Work by Cal Newport

Slow Productivity by Cal Newport

Attention Span by Gloria Mark

Hyperfocus by Chris Bailey

Essentialism by Greg McKeown

Flow by Mihaly Csikszentmihalyi

# REQUEST FOR A REVIEW

Thanks for picking up my book.

An author is a person who throws ideas into the sea of souls.

There are few people with whom the idea resonates, and then they pick it up and say kind words about the work.

These kind words lift the author to the heights of infinite solace and drown him in the sea of endorphins.

Please say a few words after reading the book.

If they are kind, then they will heal me, and if unkind, they will teach me.

But if readers are indifferent to a work, then it starts to die.

# OTHER BOOKS BY
# THE SAME AUTHOR

Easy Book of Thoughts

The book and the boy

Song of a solo man

www.ingramcontent.com/pod-product-compliance
Lightning Source LLC
Chambersburg PA
CBHW031550150726
47990CB00001B/297